COMPANIES AND COMMUNITIES:
Promoting Business Involvement in the Community

Informing policy by establishing objective facts

The Policy Studies Institute (PSI) is Britain's leading independent research organisation undertaking studies of economic, industrial and social policy, and the workings of political institutions.

PSI is a registered charity, run on a non-profit basis, and is not associated with any political party, pressure group or commercial interest.

PSI attaches great importance to covering a wide range of subject areas with its multi-disciplinary approach. The Institute's 40+ researchers are organised in teams which currently cover the following programmes:

Family Finances and Social Security
Health Studies and Social Care
Innovation and New Technology
Quality of Life and the Environment
Social Justice and Social Order
Employment Studies
Arts and the Cultural Industries
Information Policy
Education

Information about the work of PSI, and a catalogue of available books can be obtained from:

Marketing Department, PSI
100 Park Village East, London NW1 3SR

COMPANIES & COMMUNITIES:
Promoting Business Involvement in the Community

Michael Fogarty and Ian Christie

Research sponsored by the BARING FOUNDATION

The publishing imprint of the independent
POLICY STUDIES INSTITUTE
100 Park Village East, London NW1 3SR
Telephone: 071-387 2171; Fax: 071-388 0914

A CIP catalogue record of this book is available from the British Library.

1 2 3 4 5 6 7 8 9

How to obtain PSI publications
All book shop and individual orders should be sent to PSI's distributors:

BEBC Ltd
9 Albion Close, Parkstone, Bournemouth BH12 3LL.

Books will normally be despatched in 24 hours. Cheques should be made payable to BEBC Ltd.

Credit card and telephone/fax orders may be placed on the following freephone numbers:

FREEPHONE: 0800 262260   FREEFAX: 0800 262266,

Booktrade Representation (UK & Eire)
Book Representation Ltd
P O Box 17, Canvey Island, Essex SS8 8HZ

PSI Subscriptions
PSI Publications are available on subscription.
Further information from PSI's subscription agent:

Carfax Publishing Company Ltd
Abingdon Science Park, P O Box 25, Abingdon OX10 3UE

Laserset by Policy Studies Institute
Printed in Great Britain by Billing and Sons Ltd, Worcester

Contents

Acknowledgements

The research reported here was made possible by the financial support of the Baring Foundation.

We are indebted to Nicholas Baring and his colleagues at the Baring Foundation for their support and advice, and to the members of the Advisory Group established for the project. The content and conclusions presented are, however, the responsibility of the authors.

The membership of the Advisory Group was as follows:

- Nicholas Baring (chairman), Baring Foundation
- Miss Barbara Beck, Anglo-German Foundation for the Study of Industrial Society
- Elliott Bernerd, Chelsfield plc
- Robin Broadley, Baring Foundation
- Chris Bullock, Shell UK Ltd
- Robert Charleston, Department of the Environment
- Mrs Bronwen Fair, Home Office
- The Hon. Alan Hare, Per Cent Club
- Joel Joffe, Allied Dunbar Assurance plc
- The Hon. Robert Loder, Curtis Brown Group Ltd
- Bill McNie, Board of Inland Revenue
- Michael Norton, Directory of Social Change
- Sir Richard O'Brien, PSI
- G. Hayden Phillips, HM Treasury
- Dr. Susan Saxon-Harrold, Charities Aid Foundation
- Barry Till, Baring Foundation
- Simon Webley, British-North American Research Association

We are very grateful to the many individuals and organisations which generously gave their time in the course of our fieldwork in Hillingdon, Sheffield and Swindon and around the country, and to the companies which took part in our postal survey.

Finally, thanks are due to Karin Erskine and Clare Morgan at PSI who prepared the text for publication.

Overview and Proposals

The terms of reference agreed at the meeting of PSI's Advisory Group on October 2, 1989, were:

> To examine the factors internal or external to companies which influence the amount, destination, and procedures of charitable giving and community involvement by medium sized companies in Britain, and to identify obstacles to the adoption by companies of the best practice in this field.

We have used four main sources:
- existing quantitative and qualitative data on companies' giving and 'total community involvement': for Britain, particularly those brought together by the Charities Aid Foundation (CAF) and Directory of Social Change; for America, particularly those of the Conference Board;
- a re-analysis of data from EXTEL on companies' declared donations, so far as the imperfect nature of these data made this useful;
- a postal questionnaire to a sample of 300 companies (including subsidiaries) employing between 500 and 2,999. The response of 40 per cent was modest but usable: somewhat biased towards the more generous givers, but otherwise with a good spread;
- interviews with thirty companies and 46 promotional agencies at national and local level. We quickly realised that, while the main 'obstacle' to be removed is within companies – the fact that many companies have not grasped the full implications of social responsibility or enlightened self-interest for the size, direction, and management of their contribution programmes – the key to removing it is to be found outside, in the processes and agencies through which companies are or might be persuaded to understand these implications better. The main part of our interviewing programme was therefore directed to exploring these processes and agencies.

Our findings are set out in six papers.

We bring the main findings together here.

I   What companies give now

'Company giving' is taken to include all forms of non-commercial community involvement or 'community investment': gifts in cash and kind, provision of facilities, secondments or other release of staff time, sponsorships and joint promotions: whether directed to charities, to other community and welfare organisations, or to enterprise and employment agencies, environmental projects, the arts, or education and research. Paper I, though adding new material from our own surveys and interviews, essentially dots the i's and crosses the t's of what is known about company giving already.

The statistics of company giving

The statistics of company giving are incomplete and of varying value. Their deficiencies are damaging for several reasons. They reflect weaknesses in companies' own budgeting: in our survey of medium sized firms we found that very few could cost their total budget for community involvement. Lack of accurate information about what individual companies do weakens the force of example. It is important that business as a whole should get full credit for its community involvement, and at present, because of deficiencies in national statistics, it does not.

We therefore welcome the efforts of CAF, Directory of Social Change, and the Per Cent Club to encourage companies to assemble and publicise data on their contributions in a more complete and standard form: though still inevitably with a degree of arbitrariness, since, as we show below, the line between what companies do for commercial and non-commercial reasons cannot be clearly drawn. The Per Cent Club is moving towards a voluntary code of practice on publication, and we hope to see this completed in the near future. Eventually, when the code is available and experience of its working has built up, the present very restricted requirement of the Companies Act 1985 to publish charitable contributions should be amended to require fuller publication in line with the code. When this stage has been reached, we would like to see publication by the Inland Revenue of comprehensive data on companies' tax-deductible or tax-recoverable contributions broken down in line with the new Companies Act requirement.

The total amount of company giving

Enough is known, however, to show that companies already make a large contribution. Directory of Social Change's minimum estimate for 1988 is £285 million, and we show in Paper I that the actual total was certainly much larger: even without bringing in any of the £182 million spent that year on sports sponsorship, which is not always or entirely commercial. Companies' contributions grew through the 1980s at a time when the 'voluntary' income of charities from fund-raising and donations tended to stagnate. On the basis of a limited study by CAF, 40-50 per cent of the total given may have taken the form of cash donations to charity, and these, though small in relation to charities' total income, were a significant element in their 'voluntary' income. Company contributions are also, of course, of particular importance for areas like enterprise development which other types of giving may not reach.

Motives for giving

The line between commercial and non-commercial giving is often blurred, and we have not tried to draw it very precisely. Companies' motivations, as stated to us, are nearly always mixed. The reason for 'charitable giving and community involvement' which respondents to our survey of medium-sized firms stressed most strongly was 'social responsibility – need to put something back into the community', but it was clear in interviews that the motive of enlightened self-interest was almost always present as well. Even in the case of charitable giving, let alone of sponsorship, there was likely to be 'something in it for us', so that the relation between donor and receiver was at least implicitly – very explicitly, of course, in an area like sponsorship – not simply a 'gift' relationship but a partnership reflecting interdependence between the company and the community, with advantages for both. We would like to see this partnership rather than gift relationship more strongly emphasised.

The efficiency of company giving

Is company giving 'efficient' in the sense of being set at the level and directed in the way which gives the best advantage both to companies themselves and to receivers? We found many ways in which the efficiency of giving might be improved, but also that there is no simple standard to apply.

However companies are classified, by size or sector or volume of profits, there is a very wide scatter in the amount and direction of what they give: as Paper VI shows, there is no standard pattern any more than in the United States. This may and does reflect accidental and historical factors and differences in companies' efficiency in planning and managing their contribution programmes. Another and better reason for the wide scatter, however, is that companies – or, as we have found, subsidiaries within companies – are individual cases, at different stages of development, with different profitability, and operating in different product and labour markets and types of community, and what is appropriate by way of a contributions policy differs accordingly. Even if variations due to 'inefficient' giving were eliminated, there would and can be no single standard for either the level or the direction of giving suitable for prescription to all companies.

'Conventions of good practice' : overall levels of giving
We agree nevertheless with the view of the Council for Charitable Support that there can be 'conventions of good practice' which 'in time are likely to become more standard'. This is true in the first place of the overall level of giving, and in this area good progress is being made. The Per Cent Club agreed initially as a 'convention of good practice' that prosperous and established firms might be expected to spend on all forms of community contribution a minimum of half of one per cent of pre-tax profits. This standard was admittedly arbitrary – something to 'latch on to', as one informant said – but realistic, reflecting, after allowing for underestimation in the statistics of declared donations, what is achieved by around a quarter of all companies employing 500 and over (Paper I, Table 6).

As recently as the middle of the 1980s informed observers, like the respondents to a Charities Aid Foundation survey of major institutional shareholders in 1985, doubted whether per cent giving would ever take off in Britain. It has done so, however: in the first place among larger firms, but we see particular potential for smaller and local firms in the modest but significant success of the first regional Per Cent Club, in Sheffield (Paper IV). So far, 18 per cent of the medium-sized companies in our sample are Per Cent Club members, though more achieve the Per Cent Club standard. The Per Cent Club's intention from the start was to raise its standard to one per cent as experience developed and in 1990 it decided that one per cent should be encouraged: not necessarily the end of the road, considering that the minimum standard now conventional in America is two per cent. Acceptance of the Per Cent Club's convention is purely voluntary, but in Paper I we use the example of television franchises to show how in special cases the standard of giving can be reinforced in other ways, in that case effectively through contract compliance.

Guidelines for contributions management: testing companies'
performance
There are also, if not exactly conventions, at least guidelines for efficiency in the management of giving and community involvement, outlined and illustrated in documents and reports such as we list at the end of Paper I. They appear piecemeal, however, and too often do not reach their intended audience. We asked our sample of medium-sized companies about two nationally publicised sources of guidance, the *Guidelines* of the Council for Charitable Support and Directory of Social Change's *Corporate Donor's Handbook*: hardly any had used them. We would like to see a concerted effort, led perhaps by Business in the Community (BitC), to bring together the guidelines so far available and develop out of them an authoritative handbook including both general guidance and specific checklists for particular fields, like those of the Council for Industry and Higher Education (CIHE) for its own field or the guidelines of the Action Resource Centre (ARC) on secondment: and to ensure maximum diffusion and publicity for it.

Meantime, existing guidelines can at least be used to test companies' performance. They are not, of course, written on stone. Just as there are companies (including some major ones) which are unwilling to commit themselves formally to the Per Cent Club's standard but actually give at least at that level, so there are companies which apparently neglect conventional guidelines for efficient management and nevertheless run effective contribution programmes. We have met cases where a company has no formal policy on community involvement, or, if it once had one, has forgotten it, or where even a large scale budget is managed on a shoe-string: and yet these companies have programmes which are both substantial and well-directed. We have been warned of the danger of over-emphasising formality in programme management or over-centralising its control: it may be easier, we have been told, to obtain a flexible response to new local needs and initiatives through the informal procedures of small companies than through the formalised procedures of large ones.

Though, however, companies may get by without observing all the rules of good practice, or may make mistakes in applying them, these rules exist and are important. While it is true that the formalisation of policies may be overdone, a formal and specific policy on giving and community relations, going beyond mere generalities, and updated as a company's circumstances change, is still desirable as a guide for current action and a baseline for judging the case for new departures, and it is worrying that 70 per cent of the companies in our survey of medium enterprises do not have one. We do not quarrel with the emphasis that many of our respondents laid on personal and family influences in the development of their community policies – individuals' initiative, after all, as the American examples in Paper VI show, is the way in which new practice is usually born – but we have found too often that community contributions budgets are based on personal and historical accident rather than regular and up-to-date review.

We have found that programmes for giving are more likely than not to be reactive, treating appeals 'on their merits', as was often said, or even 'first come, first served'. Only a minority of the companies that we interviewed had proactive programmes: researching the field and considering new possibilities, like less popular causes or new uses for secondment (ARC's comments on deficiencies on company practice in this respect are quoted in Paper II): focussing giving so as to produce a significant impact, and monitoring results. We show below that we also found vague attitudes to the tax efficiency of giving.

In larger companies, the working relation between headquarters and managers in branches and subsidiaries on community programmes is important. We met several where this needs to be reconsidered because of over-centralisation, or alternatively the absence of a strong lead from the centre, or of an inadequate flow of information between headquarters and local management.

In small companies with limited staffs part-time management of programmes is inevitable, and can be effective provided that responsibilities are clearly assigned and accounted for – 'a real job', as one informant said – and provided that staff have opportunities for training and the exchange of experience appropriate to this field: but that is not always the case. Bearing in mind that 27 per cent of our respondent firms employed over 2,000, we might have hoped that more than 7.5 per cent would have at least one manager dealing with community affairs full-time. An informant with particularly wide experience commented that:

> There is obvious scope for both the training and the accreditation of community involvement staff on a more concerted basis. Any effort here should also address the problem of who is best to be appointed to such posts and what experience is required.

Specific suggestions included more appointments from the voluntary sector, secondments of company staff for experience before taking up a community affairs appointment, and net-working with experienced community affairs managers from leading companies, perhaps with the creation of a formal professional association.

There are limits to what can be expected of small and especially part-time community relations staffs, especially when it comes to researching the field of appeals and ensuring the best value for money for donors and receivers, but also ways of at least partly overcoming these, for example through delegation to company trusts or use of intermediaries like Councils of Voluntary Service or community trusts: but the use made of these proved to be patchy.

We have met companies which systematically promote employee giving and volunteering and involve employees closely in their contributions programmes, including delegation of much of their programme to employee-run charities, and have been impressed with the value of this to companies, in terms of staff development and cohesion, as well as to employees themselves. But we have more often met what might be called vague benevolence – casual and occasional encouragement – towards activities of this kind.

The size of the cake. Barriers to giving more?

Better management could certainly achieve better value for money in many companies' community involvement, but is this within the existing level of giving, or could companies be expected to give more? Can the size of the cake be increased?

There has been some recent tendency for giving by the largest company donors to plateau, and we have noted fears that, as the 'appeals mountain' grows and new claimants such as TECs arrive, demands on companies are reaching a level at which, given their present overall levels of contribution, some causes may be crowded out: particularly charitable causes, but also for example contributions to enterprise agencies. Companies' willingness to give is in any case broadly linked to the level of pretax profits, and a downturn could substantially affect it.

The qualification about 'present overall levels of contribution' is important. The processes by which new levels and patterns of giving are promoted need time to operate (Paper II) in the UK as in the USA (Paper VI), but the Per Cent Club, as just said, already sees justification for moving its standard up from one half to one per cent. Whatever the speed of progress towards enlarging the cake, nothing in our evidence suggests that there are insuperable barriers in the way: and, as and when it happens, there is a large potential for increased donations from most even of today's larger and more generous donors, let alone the rest.

We tested this in various ways. In one of our case studies we asked company informants to look around them and see whether they could name other companies in the area which are established, profitable, and substantial, yet not, so far, significantly involved in contributing to the community and could reasonably be expected to do more: they had no difficulty in drawing up a list. We asked the medium-sized companies in our survey about factors which might restrict growth in their giving in future. Only one factor, 'financial position of the enterprise', was generally seen as 'very important', and the importance which companies attached to this and most other factors in reply to a hypothetical question tended to evaporate when explored in interviews with reference to their own experience. One exception, which refers less to companies themselves than to presentation by receivers, was 'lack of information on charities'.

Among the factors whose importance evaporated in this way was 'opposition from shareholders'. There were few references in company interviews to either negative or positive reactions from shareholders: one view was that it would be a pleasure, from the angle of community affairs staff, if shareholders were better informed and could be persuaded to react more. CAF found in its survey of major institutional shareholders in 1985 that the level of giving at which they might become worried about undue diversion of shareholders' funds was typically well above that even of CAF's Top 50 donors, that none could recall a case of actually being worried about 'excessive' giving, and that many of them had seen no need to inform themselves accurately about this area at all. A director of one of these institutions confirmed CAF's picture up to date.

Carrying the message

Companies contribute a great deal – more than the available national statistics give them credit for – and have been increasing their giving while others have been slowing down. Moreover, nothing that we have said should be taken as a criticism of the individual competence of those who administer companies' community programmes. We were impressed with the quality of the company officers whom we interviewed and with the competence and common sense of their detailed management: but too often they were managing in a limited and unsatisfactory context. Guidelines which companies could use to reappraise the general levels of their contributions policies or to give them a sharper edge are available, but too often, in the range of companies with which we have been particularly concerned, the message has not got through. Papers II-V set out to answer the question: how can it be delivered more effectively?

II National promotion

The question about 'removing obstacles' becomes at this point one of marketing. There is out there a market for more, and more efficient, company giving. It is a market of individual customers, since every company is a case on its own, with its own interests and potential. While all methods of marketing may be relevant and are used, the common consent of our informants is that the approach in the end has to be one to one, reaching key decision makers in individual companies on the basis of each company's situation and interests: and a great deal depends on building personal networks, locally as well as nationally, with the right movers and shakers (we prefer 'catalysts') at their centre. Paper II reviews the existing national promotional agencies, and the three case study papers (III-V) consider promotional action at local level.

Till a few years ago, the question might have been how to get national promotion of the 'culture of giving' going and fill some of its obvious gaps. There was a time when CAF, the oldest of the promotional agencies, was almost alone in the field. Since the 1970s, however, the scene has been transformed. More and more agencies have entered the field: general purpose, like Business in the Community; specialised, like the Per Cent Clubs or the agencies promoting secondments and volunteering from the workplace, arts or 'social' sponsorship, enterprise, employment of disadvantaged groups, environmental improvement, or education-industry links, alongside the continuing concern of CAF for efficient and tax-efficient giving; information services, like those of Directory of Social Change as well as CAF; or action to promote integrated local leadership, as through Common Purpose's community leadership programmes. The government has made a large input of its own through general encouragement of the culture of giving, through grants and tax incentives, and through the partnership spinoff from its own action agencies, including the inner city agencies and Training and Enterprise Councils. There has been notable leadership from the Royal family, and especially from the Prince of Wales.

The question today is no longer about the range of promotional efforts: it would be hard to name a field of promotion without one or more agencies at work. Nor, in general, is it about the way in which agencies go about their work. Agencies like BitC, ARC, or Association for British Sponsorship of the Arts (ABSA) modify and develop their strategy as they go along, and sometimes make mistakes and have to revise it: but in general the way in which they go about promotion corresponds to the rules just suggested, which are in fact derived from their experience. For that reason we have not gone into possible improvements in the work of individual agencies in detail. We make, however, more general and strategic points about the finance of national promotion, its structure, its information and ideological base, and the role of the government.

Finance: money for marketing, matching grants, and tax incentives
On the finance of national promotion we have one surprisingly negative and two more positive findings, one of which is central to our recommendations.

Tax incentives
One of the surprises of this study has been the limited importance which nearly all our company informants, when asked about 'removing obstacles', attached to further improvement in tax incentives for corporate giving. Community affairs managers were certainly aware of the need for tax-efficiency, though sometimes rather vaguely so ('we leave it to the accounts department' or references to 'incomprehensible literature'). But we had repeatedly the impression that this was not a central consideration in their thinking about the development of their companies' community policies. As a spokesman for an enterprise agency said: in talking to firms, I have learnt to put tax incentives last. And, so far as giving by companies as such was concerned, our informants were almost unanimous that new tax incentives are not a high priority.

Perhaps companies' answers would have been different if we had questioned them before the considerable improvement of tax incentives since the 1970s, which have brought incentives in Britain to a level comparable to what international companies meet in the United States. Perhaps again the rather off-hand attitude to tax incentives which we met reflected the more general casualness of contributions management in many companies. One informant commented that the point about a comparison between British and American tax incentives is not that they are widely different, which they are not, but that American managers and especially accountants tend to talk about them differently, as a business proposition to be discussed in a businesslike way in the context not only of a company's contributions programme but of its whole business plan. For some informants, 'incomprehensible literature' about tax-efficiency was a problem. The new and simplified procedure for giving through Gift Aid is an important improvement here. There are well-known grey areas, for the purposes of the Revenue, between what is clearly commercial and a business expense and what is clearly tax-deductible as a donation: guides like the *Corporate Donor's Handbook* point to ways through these areas, but that guide happens, as we found, not to be much used.

Whatever the reasons, the main impression was clear. Tax incentives, old or new, were for our company informants a rather marginal consideration, and the main point for action appeared to be not so much to develop new incentives as to sharpen awareness of those which exist, and of their value to receivers even more than to donors: a problem of perception and of the marketing of incentives rather than of incentives in themselves.

This impression was reinforced by what was said about payroll giving: let us call it, as in common usage, by the title of CAF's scheme, Give As You Earn (GAYE). On the order of priority when promoting employee giving, a personnel manager used an analogy with covenanting for church collections. The first step is for the vicar to work up the congregation on the reasons for giving: then the churchwarden may incidentally add that, if you put the money in a covenant envelope and sign the form at the end of the year, the parish gets one third more.

We were told repeatedly that there are two reasons why GAYE has taken off more slowly than had been hoped, and these reasons illustrate not only why informants tended to put its tax incentive aspect on the back burner but why our own priority, if new money is available, would be not for new tax incentives but for putting more resources into 'marketing' good practice to companies.

Firstly, purely individual giving through GAYE is 'boring', 'unexciting', hard to promote and with a tendency to low take-up even where a real effort is made: by contrast with the 'fun' and widespread participation in employees' collective fund-raising efforts for a targeted and popular cause. The collective/targeted and individual approaches can be combined by targeting GAYE to particular causes in the context of an employee fund-raising drive, and we have met cases where this has been done with success: but GAYE in itself tends to be seen as 'boring'.

Secondly, the input of time, effort, and money needed to get a scheme like this off the ground was greatly underestimated. An unexpected level of start-up costs has had to be met, and many of both companies and potential receivers have found the effort not worth while.

Both these points, it can be seen, are about marketing GAYE – one about the right design for a marketing campaign, the other about resources for marketing – rather than about its existing tax incentive, or possible improvements in it like those proposed by CAF and quoted in Paper II.

This report is about corporate rather than family or household giving, but the two may be connected. One comment about the United States was that American corporate decision makers live, as individuals, in a culture where the habit of budgeting for giving, as distinct from giving out of the margin left over when the rest of a family's needs and interests are provided for, is more widespread than in Britain: this, it was suggested, carries over into the way they in which they look at corporate giving. CAF and the Council for Charitable Support have launched the Windsor Group to promote the budgeting approach as a long-term change in the culture of British households. It is an interesting hypothesis that this will in the end carry over into managers' attitudes to corporate giving, but evidently one which will be verified only in the long or very long run.

Matching grants

The incentive effect of matching grants emerged much more clearly than that of tax incentives. For governmental grants, the success of the Business Sponsorship Incentive Scheme in the arts is an outstanding example. CAF has shown that matching grants can be a very effective way to stimulate promotional agencies to develop their own capacity. We have seen in our case studies the enthusiastic response of community trusts to CAF's competition for 'challenge grants', based on American finance and to be matched £2 for £1 from local funding, to start trusts on the way to a substantial endowment yielding a regular and reliable flow of income. A number of the companies which we interviewed, and 23 per cent of those in our sample of medium-sized companies, make matching grants to encourage employee fund raising: sometimes casually and at discretion, but sometimes on a more regular basis. In one company, which had made an early and at least modest success of GAYE, linked to an employee-run charitable trust, we were left wondering how far this success was due to GAYE's own rather modest tax incentive or to the fact that the company not only has mobilised a collective effort by employees but matches their donations £ for £: so that, as the company magazine points out, £7.50 a month from the employee means £20 a month to the charity. The potential and cost of matching grants needs to be explored further than we have been able to do.

Money for marketing
Our main financial point, however, is about 'money for marketing'. If more money is available for promoting the culture of corporate giving in Britain, whether from business, foundations, or the government, our evidence shows that the best payback is likely to come from strengthening the resources and especially the staffing of the promotional agencies.

We have been impressed with the increase in recent years in the resources put into marketing company giving, in terms of money as well as of effort and time: informants used graphic language to describe the hard work entailed in an individual and customised approach to not always very receptive companies ('the door is not open – it has to be pushed'). But we have found one area after another – in the arts, in promoting volunteering from the workplace, in developing community trusts or community leadership programmes or in catalysing business leadership outside the government's priority action areas, as well as the case just mentioned of starting up GAYE – where promotional activities are underresourced, and the injection of quite small sums could make a large difference to agencies' capacity to get around to companies and bring them into the net. Even the bigger national agencies are by comparison with any substantial business very small scale: still more, to look forward, the agencies which work at local level. We see more money for direct reinforcement of the marketing effort as a high priority: whether it comes from business, from trusts and foundations, or from local or central government. We would like to see BitC promote a working group from the relevant agencies to explore further where and how action might best be taken.

The structure of national promotion: general and specialised agencies and the role of Business in the Community
The number and variety of national agencies now engaged in promoting the 'culture of giving' is bewildering. Many have their fingers in more than one pie, and many pies have more than one finger in them. It is not surprising that many of our informants were less than clear about who does and should do what or about the need for all of them.

The existence of many promotional agencies with specialised fields of competence is an advantage rather than otherwise: Adam Smith's views on the division of labour are as valid here as anywhere else, and a degree of competition between agencies is creative. This, however, is provided that the division of labour is clear, the road to the right agency is well signposted, and attention is paid to the general development of the system of promotion as well as to that of particular specialisms within it. The Public Accounts

Committee has recently called for better liaison between the departments and agencies responsible for the government's *Action for Cities* programme, while recognising – this also emerged in seminars given at PSI in 1988/9 by Sir Leon Brittan – the difficulties in the way of a single centralised master plan. A number of our own informants fastened particularly on what they saw as confusion over the division of responsibilities between BitC and other more specialised agencies.

BitC covers a very wide field and achieves results largely through or in cooperation with others. It is not surprising that its image therefore tends to be blurred. BitC has recently taken steps to clarify its image and to sort out its relationship with some specialised agencies, as with the formation of the Bridge Group which links it to a number of voluntary agencies promoting business action on employment and the environment. Some of our informants argued, however, that there is more here than an image problem and that the sorting out process needs to be carried further. BitC, they suggest, has on the one hand been duplicating what might better be done by specialised agencies, and on the other falling short in its role of general promotion and signposting. They see the general role on which it should be concentrating as including, in summary:

- general 'consciousness-raising' among companies on community involvement, as in BitC's current national campaign to interest medium and small enterprises;
- a central focus for information about business involvement and best practice, and action to ensure that this information is collected – whether by BitC itself or by others – and is easily available and diffused;
- taking action to fill gaps in the networks of promotional networks at either national or local level and to ensure that resources are found for them;
- acting as a national forum and lobby on behalf of the whole complex of promotional agencies.

BitC does in fact do these things: its campaign to reach medium and small enterprises is certainly an example of consciousness-raising, and its promotion of Business Leadership Teams and many of the activities of its Target Teams are equally certainly cases of filling gaps. The argument is, however, that it could do them better and more comprehensively if it committed more of its limited resources to activities within its general role and left others to specialist agencies: BitC's principal responsibility should be to start things off and back them up. Paper II shows that there is justification for this argument and that the division of responsibilities between BitC and the specialised agencies does need further clarification.

Information and ideology: consolidating the theory of corporate giving

We have recommended above improvement in the statistics of companies' community involvement and the development and diffusion of an authoritative set of guidelines or 'conventions of good practice' on the management of companies' community programmes. Another issue mentioned by our informants was the need for fuller and more accessible information about 'best practice'. The Per Cent Club exists among other things to promote the exchange of experience between companies, but a comment from within the Club is that there is a shortage of easily available 'ammunition' – records and examples of good practice – to use in company contacts. PSI has been commissioned by the Department of the Environment to collect some of this 'ammunition' from three cities, with special reference to inner city areas. BitC may or may not be itself the best agency to collect material of that kind, but it should certainly be part of BitC's general purpose remit to ensure that it is collected, easily available, and diffused.

There is also, however, a wider issue. It has been put to us that for many prosperous and established companies the financing of present or even increased contributions to the community is, if not exactly 'peanuts', as one informant said, at least a rather marginal consideration, and that what they chiefly need is 'reasons' why they should contribute to the community.

One sort of reason is the experience of other companies, with examples of the advantage of good practice to companies and to receivers. There can also, however, be reasons of a wider kind. There is now a great deal of experience to quote and a great deal of thinking behind it, expressed in the policy statements of a number of leading companies. What we have not found is any general effort, or even many particular efforts, by management schools and institutions to consolidate this into a general theory of companies' responsibility in the community, in a situation where demands on companies are increasing and confusing and a clear basis for 'reasoning' is essential, and to incorporate this into the teaching and practice of management: something more than practical guidelines, and treating the community contributions function not as a marginal issue but as part of companies' general business plan. Business ethics in a rather different sense, for example the ethics of financial markets, are acquiring a new emphasis in business studies, but this is not true of corporate responsibility in the community.

Ideologies are powerful: as Keynes used to point out, the practical man is usually the servant of some theorist long dead. In the present case what is needed is a theorist still to come. America, as Paper VI shows, has had the advantage of a more generally accepted ideology of corporate responsibility than Britain. We identify below some other roles which universities and business schools can play, but there is one here which should be among the basics of their programmes of management studies, and we would like to see them take it up.

The national climate and what is expected by and from government

We show in Paper II the large contribution which the government has made to promoting the culture of corporate giving in Britain. In Paper VI we show from American as well as British experience how this can be and has been helped by the creation and maintenance of the right national climate in the sense of turning away from overreliance on government and accenting the contributions of the private and voluntary sectors and of ensuring opportunities for good profitability. From both countries, however, there is a warning. American and British experience concur that, while companies may be ready to do more in a climate of that kind, this does not imply that they either wish to or even could take over what are seen as government's regular responsibilities. The priorities of companies remain those of companies, not the government, and one company informant after another expressed strong objection to the idea that business might be expected to take over in areas like education or health what they see as properly the responsibilities of government: which they perceived as already happening, at least at the margin.

What is and is not the responsibility of government cannot be precisely defined, but we would like to see the government reinforce as strongly and precisely as possible the statements of John Patten and other ministers that the intention is indeed that business should add something where government leaves off ('the icing on the cake', as was sometimes light-heartedly said) rather than replace the government's own role.

We add another more marginal point about how the state for its part defines the responsibilities of companies in the community. None of our informants suggested that *ultra vires* is a significant obstacle to company giving. The old legal ruling that 'there are to be no cakes and ale except such as are for the shareholders' benefit' can be and has been stretched a long way. But there were one or two references to *ultra vires*, and we think it worth considering, when opportunity offers, laying it to rest with a General Purposes Clause in the Companies Acts to bring British into line with American law: to the effect, as George Goyder has proposed, that companies have a general power to act towards the community 'in as responsible a manner as would be expected from a responsible citizen in the like circumstances'.

III-V The local case studies

Our three local case study areas (Papers III-V) were chosen for their differences. Sheffield is a city with a strong traditional identity where minds have been focussed by severe problems over the run-down of traditional industries. Swindon has seen the disappearance of its traditional economic base, but offset by a rapid expansion of other industries and services in a favoured position on the M4 corridor. It has lost its old identity but is well on the way to developing a new one, facing on the way the problems of growth and development. Hillingdon is prosperous, but, as local people tend to say, is hardly in itself a place at all: a slice of North London, still in many ways an artificial assembly of older communities, definable in terms of local government but with no natural focus either geographically or because of dramatic problems of economic disaster or explosive growth.

The pattern of business involvement reflects these differences. In all three cities many companies are in fact involved with and contributing to the community, at all levels from the 'cosy' relationship (as it was called in one of them) of an individual company to a particular charity or school to participation in larger collective efforts. But whereas in Sheffield there is almost a surplus of strategic initiatives for the city's regeneration ('not another initiative!'), in Hillingdon business networks or business-public sector partnerships have to be looked for. As a local government officer said: 'It's the Hillingdon way: everyone does his own thing'. Swindon comes in between: there are gaps in its promotional networks, as Paper III shows, but there is effective and developing leadership both from business and from the public sector.

Two things, however, are common to the three cities: all have problems to whose solution companies have a contribution to make, and in none of them has companies' potential for contribution yet been fully realised. The case studies illustrate the range of possible contributions by way of investment, local recruitment or purchasing, support for enterprise agencies or for infra-structural development, including housing and traffic problems; partnership in education and training, or support for community development, voluntary social social services, or the arts. When what companies do contribute to these problems is compared to what they might, there is a gap, or more accurately, as Paper III shows, a J-shaped curve, with some companies and individual business leaders very actively involved, but, except in the case of school-business contacts, involvement tails rapidly away among the rest. How, therefore, might local promotion of companies' community involvement be organised to better effect?

'Conventions of good practice' for local promotion
There are no clearly agreed 'conventions of good practice' for local promotion of companies' community involvement, but there could be, and there is a role in developing and applying them for national as well as local agencies. All the national agencies which we have reviewed are in their own ways reaching down to local level and to medium or small enterprises, but this does not yet contribute as much as it might to a coherent pattern of local promotion. BitC's local Business Leadership Teams could be extended not only to obvious priority areas but to others, like Hillingdon, whose problems are less obvious and yet there are large opportunities for the sort of leadership that the teams provide. CAF's programme for promoting community trusts and Common Purpose's community leadership programmes are still at an early stage of development. CAF and Directory of Social Change bring into focus national information on companies' involvement, but have not yet gone on to promote the establishment of local data bases. The way in which business-education links have been developed provides a good model. School-business links are one of the strongest areas of company involvement, and this has been due not only to 'mobilising the customers' locally but to the national drive behind the programme.

Recognising diversity
As before, we begin with a warning about the dangers of overformalisation. The differences between the three cities point to an important though negative conclusion. There is no case for trying to impose a grand design for local promotion of the 'culture of giving' on all communities alike. The approach to companies has to be the same at the local as at the national level, customised, one to one, using whatever formal or informal networks come to hand. We agree with the Swindon informant, himself at the centre of the local networks, who said that what is likely to be effective for this purpose is not a 'monolithic' approach but the use of 'a number of

vehicles...to ease companies into the contributions scenario', and to encourage them to make their contributions in the most effective way. These 'vehicles', however, will not everywhere be the same, and the best way to go about developing and using them depends on local circumstances. Leadership may come from many sources, often by personal accident: 'a personal crusade', one Hillingdon leader said of his own commitment, but he became aware of his 'crusade' by the accident of cooption to a local business-public sector partnership. Nominally similar agencies may have very different potential in different places: the same degree of leadership cannot reasonably be expected from the five small and very local Chambers of Commerce in Hillingdon as from the Chamber of Commerce in Sheffield. Established spheres of influence or old antagonisms have to be taken into account or worked round, and these again vary from place to place.

Nevertheless, though we cannot say that there are established 'conventions of good practice' for organising local promotion, there certainly could be: there may not be one ideal pattern of local promotion, but there are conditions which any effective pattern needs to meet. None of our case studies provides a perfect model, but between them they point towards a number of guidelines.

A structured and collective approach: informality is necessary but not enough

The approach to companies at local level is, as just said, no different from that found to be effective by the national agencies reviewed in Paper II. It has in the end to be individual, tailored to each company's interests and potential, and relying very much on personal contacts and informal networks. As was said in Sheffield, 'You go and ask your friend Jack', using the informal grapevines of 'Britain's biggest village'.

Informality, however, is not enough. Our Swindon case study shows how informal involvement of companies through the 'mafia' needs to be and is supplemented with more formal action like Thamesdown Arts' recruitment campaign, the brokering of school-business links by Wiltshire County Council's INDEL unit, or the at least semi-formal activities of the Swindon Partnership: and how local voluntary organisations have come to see that an effective approach to local businesses needs a highly profiled and well-resourced focus in the shape of an endowed community trust. Our Sheffield case study illustrates the value of backing individual approaches to companies with a strategic vision – perhaps in Sheffield one should say 'visions' – of local problems and possibilities, and with a variety of forms of collective action and partnership between the private and public sectors. The Hillingdon case study illustrates how much may be lost where collective and formal action is underdeveloped, and the situation there may well be typical of what would be found in other areas whose problems are not of obvious priority.

A common information base

Locally as well as nationally, it is important for determining priorities, planning future action, and attracting companies' interest and involvement that it should be generally known what are the problems to which business might be contributing and what is being done to meet them. A good deal of information does circulate in our three cities, and we do not under-estimate the effectiveness of the exchanges which take place not only in formal meetings but through informal networks like the 'Swindon mafia'. Our impression, however, is that few even of those business, voluntary sector, or local authority people who are actively engaged in the three cities see the whole picture. A more deliberate effort is needed to fill this gap by bringing information together, updating it as new issues are raised and new emphases appear – like the emergence of 'social regeneration' alongside economic regeneration in the recent history of Sheffield – and ensuring its diffusion through reports and publications, forums or 'mafias', and the media.

We do not specify who should take the lead in creating a comprehensive local data base and diffusing its information: that depends on local circumstances. There is an obvious and central role for local authorities, but the lead might equally be taken by a local university or polytechnic, a business group or public-private sector partnership, a TEC, or even an individual lead firm. What is important is that action should be taken to ensure that it is done, and here as elsewhere we see a role for national as well as local agencies. CAF and Directory of Social Change do not provide local information services, but might well take a lead in promoting them. So might BitC. One of its target teams has made a start with a proposal to promote a regional information service on the activities and needs of voluntary organisations, for the guidance particularly of small and medium enterprises which do not have the resources to research the field themselves.

For the longer run, we see a large potential in Common Purpose's idea (Paper II) of creating a receptive audience through community leadership training programmes. The intention of these programmes is to build up over the years in each community a cadre of leaders and future leaders from the private, public, and voluntary sectors who have trained together over a year to appreciate the range of problems in their community, and then remain in contact as a growing network of 'graduates'. An incidental advantage, as community leadership programmes spread, is that when their graduates move to other areas they may be able to slot in immediately to the corresponding 'graduate' group in their new community. Community leadership programmes are now well tried and established in America (Paper VI). In Britain they are still at an early stage of development: we would like to see their rapid extension.

Developing and financing local promotional networks

The formal and informal networks and partnerships on which so much depends in local promotion neither will nor should be the same everywhere, but there are several general points for which to watch.

Are there well-focussed networks and structures?

The first is simply that there must be networks and structures, and that these need to include strong focal institutions for the business and voluntary sectors, working in partnership with each other and with the public sector: where they are weak or do not exist, they must be developed. Sheffield as has been said is almost overrun with business and business-public sector initiatives, yet still with weaknesses. Too much has been expected of a small group of business leaders. 'Social regeneration' tended till recently to be underemphasised, and a new grouping has been created to remedy this. In Hillingdon, by contrast, the networks are underdeveloped, and we have suggested, for the business side, that there is a role for BitC in remedying this: though with a warning from experience in Sheffield that intervention by an outside body like BitC needs a high degree of tact.

In all three cities there are weaknesses on the side of voluntary organisations. Business informants were often bewildered by the number and variety of these organisations: the voluntary sector, some thought, is too diverse, overlapping, and confusing ('for every cause there are five organisations') and needs to rationalise itself. That, however, is to misunderstand what voluntary organisations are about. Certainly there are cases for rationalisation, like those quoted in Paper V of arts and old people's welfare associations in Hillingdon, but we do not see a general drive for rationalisation as either necessary or desirable. The voluntary sector is precisely what its name implies, and multiplicity and polycentricity are a consequence of this with which it is necessary to live.

The point is rather that the voluntary sector needs to be signposted for companies' guidance and to have visible focusses and points of reference. Councils of Voluntary Service can fill this role if they are well enough resourced, but in cities like Hillingdon and Swindon they are not. One answer, obviously, is to give them more resources: as was pointed out in Hillingdon, even one extra part-time member of staff could have made a large difference. Another is to supplement them with other focal institutions, and here CAF's drive to promote community trusts is relevant.

A community trust can act as a high-profile broker for company giving and source of information on opportunities for it: as a promoter of efficiency in giving for the benefit particularly of smaller enterprises and voluntary organisations whose own resources for managing a contribution programme or developing their approach to business are limited: and as a flywheel in the system by which company contributions reach the voluntary sector. Companies change their priorities for giving, 'donor fatigue' sets in, and companies in any case tend to be more interested in funding projects than in 'core' funding for organisations' administration and overheads. A central channel for donations and a regular flow of endowment income can enable gaps to be filled.

All three of our cities have community trusts or foundations, of a different and changing kind. Looking at the national picture (Paper II), it is likely to be some years before community trusts or foundations become as widespread as they are in America and their pattern of activities settles down. At present they have a mixed pattern, with different and in some cases (like the South Yorkshire Trust) changing emphases on the one hand on building an endowment or on the other on 'federated giving', raising current donations and passing them through on the lines of the American United Way. Both these approaches need to be pursued, whether, in each locality, separately or under a single roof. CAF is focussing at present, for good reasons, on the example of American endowed foundations, but without overlooking the possibilities of local federated giving for the future. The potential of United Way's model of a comprehensive approach to local federated giving is clear from American experience, but has been too little appreciated in Britain, and we have included United Way International's own account of how a local United Way operates as an appendix to Paper VI.

Catalysts

If there is to be no imposed grand design for local promotion of the culture of giving, then skills in catalysing action among and between the many relevant and independent, sometimes jealously independent, 'vehicles' are vital: whether in bringing appropriate networks into existence or in ensuring that they mesh effectively together. Catalysing is a delicate art – how is action to be secured without overriding expected spheres of influence or expecting to get all the credit? – and the style which is appropriate will differ in different places. We would, for example, expect a BitC Business Leadership Team to apply a more direct style of leadership in an area like Hillingdon which, so far as leadership at that level is concerned, is a nearly virgin field, than in one like Sheffield where it is necessary to tread softly among many existing initiatives.

Who are or should be the catalysts? In a sense the answer must be that they come from wherever they come from. It may be a case of a lead firm, like Allied Dunbar in Swindon, or of individuals who step out of the ranks of business, as in Sheffield, or of the council officers who promoted the Hillingdon Partnership Trust. Initiatives may come from a business organisation like BitC, a local authority, or a government action agency. There are certainly some institutions which could play a larger part. We have been impressed with the potential for leadership of Brunel and Sheffield Universities – of Brunel's business clubs, for example – but it has not so far been directed to the problems of the community as distinct from those of the universities' own development.

Whoever the catalysts are and wherever they come from, they have to be looked for: we strongly underline that leadership in creating and operating local networks has to be catalysed rather than imposed or directed. The role of Allied Dunbar in Swindon is a good illustration. It is by common consent the lead firm in the city so far as community involvement is concerned, and one with a wide influence, but it is also deliberately cautious about pressing its leadership role too strongly or directly.

Money for marketing

Finally, what we have said above about money for marketing at national level applies equally to marketing the 'culture of giving' at local level. Approaching and convincing firms is a time-consuming operation, and we have noted through the three case studies example after example of where an additional staff member, or even one part or full time staff member where there are none already, or perhaps the substitution of regularly employed staff for secondees who can give good service but over short periods and with a loss of continuity when they change, could make a large difference to the impact of local promotional agencies. It is not only time for approaching firms which is needed: some agencies are too overrun with routine and development work to be able to think and plan strategically. We found the need for modest extra staffing both in voluntary social service agencies like the Hillingdon Association for Voluntary Service, which is too understaffed even to keep fully in touch with its members or potential members, or the Thamesdown Community Trust, and in business-centred organisations like some enterprise agencies or, in Sheffield, the regional Per Cent Club.

VI   Learning from America

Was British industry on the mean side compared with the Americans? He thought not, just that the idea had not been marketed here, whereas in America, businessmen had long sold the notion to each other and corporate giving was widely accepted.
(Interview with Sir Mark Weinberg, *Observer magazine*, July 8, 1990.)

The material brought together in Paper VI shows that Sir Mark Weinberg's comment hits the point exactly. American companies, in America, do on the average contribute to their communities several times as much as British companies. Yet America is not basically different: the 'culture of giving' has been marketed there in essentially the same ways which prove successful in Britain, only it has been marketed for longer.

We concentrate in Paper VI on the process by which the culture of giving in American corporations has been and is being developed, and make four main points.

First, in America as in Britain there is no standard pattern of company giving: still less can it be assumed that American corporations will carry their pattern of giving with them when they operate in other cultures. American like British experience shows that companies are always an individual case and that the message about corporate giving must be tailored accordingly.

Secondly, the message passes in America as in Britain primarily through one-to-one contacts and personal networks, though supported in due course by larger-scale organisation and promotion. The history of marketing the culture of giving in the USA is very much about personal and small-group catalysts 'selling the notion to each other'. American experience adds, however, the qualification that reliance on individual and personal contacts for spreading the message is not a reason for thinking small: plan adequate budgets, as an American informant said, and go to the top to finance them. We have shown in Paper II how American influence has lifted CAF's thinking about the scale on which to start community trusts into a new dimension.

Thirdly, national policies and influences do nevertheless count, and not only in ways such as clarification of the law on corporations' right to donate or the development of tax incentives. The switch away from 'big government' in America as in Britain from the end of the 1970s towards greater emphasis on private and voluntary sector initiatives created a new climate for company giving and led – along with, and in so far as there were, improved profit margins – to a large increase in the volume of giving and to the start or acceleration of a number of specific initiatives. Several of these – Per Cent Clubs, community leadership programmes, community foundations, organised volunteering from the workplace, or partnership in urban regeneration – are now being followed up in Britain as some earlier American developments like the United Way were not.

Again, however, there is a qualification, already mentioned in considering the attitudes of British firms. The new surge of corporate giving in America is not to be understood as meaning that American any more than British companies have been interested in taking over the regular responsibilities of government. They could not have done so, seeing the small size of even American corporate contributions by comparison with government expenditure. But in any case data of what and where they give show that their priorities have remained their own, and different from those of government. They responded to the new climate, but by joining in doing a number of things which the federal and local governments were perceived either as not doing or as not doing well.

Fourthly, there is a double-edged message, though with a happy ending, about the speed at which the 'culture of giving' can be developed. The bad news is that the American culture of giving has taken a very long time to grow, with a history stretching back to before the first World War. In the 1930s tax-deductible donations by US corporations, as a percentage of pre-tax profits, were only a quarter to onethird of what they are now. The good news, however, is that once the foundations have been laid, and if the conditions become right, development can as in the 1980s be very rapid: and there is reason to think that this is exactly the situation which we have in Britain today. It is notable how rapidly new initiatives in American corporate giving in the last ten to fifteen years have been taken up in Britain, and an unfortunate accident of history that the main development of the United Way dates back to a time before Britain was ready to receive its message.

We have concentrated on lessons from America because that was where the most relevant – and, so far as the UK is concerned, the most copied – experience has hitherto been. In future, however, experience from continental Europe will become increasingly relevant as European integration proceeds. We welcome the initiative of a group including Directory of Social Change, Allied Dunbar, American Express, and the Centre for Employment Initiatives, which is preparing a report on company giving across the member states of the European Community.

Summary and points for action

We have stressed how much companies already do for the community, over and above their central role in creating wealth and employment: and there are many features of the present arrangements for marketing community involvement to companies which we would not wish to change, because what is done is being done well or at least developing in the right direction. We have been impressed with the rapid growth of promotional action since the 1970s, the wide range of promotional agencies, and their generally clear grasp of the need for a one to one, customised, approach to companies in their different circumstances. But there is room for further development under several heads.

National statistics and illustrations of 'best practice'

1. [pp.ii] CAF, Directory of Social Change, and the Per Cent Club are promoting fuller and more accurate statistics of the whole range of companies' community involvement. We would like to see this lead as soon as possible to a voluntary code of practice, eventually providing the basis for a wider and more detailed requirement to declare donations under the Companies Acts, and for comprehensive data on companies' tax-deductible and tax-recoverable contributions, broken down in line with the new requirement, from the Inland Revenue. [p.xv] We also note the call by some informants for a better supply of 'ammunition' – illustrations of best practice – for approaches to companies, and the suggestion that BitC might take the lead in this.

Company practice

2. [p.iii] Companies' motives even for charitable giving nearly always include an element of 'enlightened self-interest' as well as of 'social responsibility'. We welcome the tendency for understanding of the relation between givers and receivers in giving to charities and community causes to change from a pure 'gift' relationship to one of partnership and mutual dependence, with advantages to both sides.

3. [p.iii-iv] Companies are individual cases, operating in different circumstances, and no single pattern of giving can be prescribed for all of them: but there can still be conventions of good practice applicable particularly to established and profitable firms.

4. [p.iv] As regards the overall level of giving, the Per Cent Club's drive to establish an arbitrary but realistic convention – initially half of one per cent of pre-tax profits, but with the intention of raising the standard as experience develops – has taken off unexpectedly well. For medium and small enterprises we see particular possibilities in the development of local Per Cent Clubs as illustrated in our Sheffield case study.

5. [p.v] There are published guidelines for company practice in the management of community programmes, but they are not well enough known or followed. BitC might again lead in bringing them together into an authoritative handbook, including both general principles and detailed check-lists for particular fields, and ensuring its wide diffusion.

6. [pp.v-vii] While our interviews have shown that guidelines should be interpreted flexibly and that there can be dangers in over-formalisation, interviews and our survey of medium-sized companies have shown a number of ways in which the existing practice of many companies clearly falls short. These include lack of formal, specific and updated policies on community involvement; reactive rather than proactive policies; weaknesses in budgeting, in the working relationship between headquarters and field management, in staffing arrangements and use of outside advice or intermediaries, and in companies' approach to employee involvement; and sometimes vagueness over tax-efficiency. We draw attention to and support the comments reported on page vi on the training and qualification of community affairs staff and networking by them.

7. [p.vii-viii] The 'restrictions' on an eventual further increase in companies' level of giving, like that envisaged by the Per Cent Clubs, which some of our respondents foresaw in reply to a hypothetical question tended to evaporate when explored in the light of companies'

actual experience. In particular, the level of giving at which major shareholders might become seriously 'worried' is well above that now found among most even of major donors.

8. [p.ix] 'Removing obstacles to company giving' becomes in the end a matter of marketing. The message about good practice exists, but has not yet been delivered to companies with full effect, and the main thrust of this report is on ways in which it might be delivered better.

National promotion of company involvement

9. [pp.ix-x] There are now national promotional agencies in all the main fields of promotion, and in general with a sound understanding of how to go about their work. Where gaps till recently existed, we show in Paper II that they are being filled. The need now is to build further improvements on this foundation.

10. [p.x-xii] There was surprising unanimity among our respondents that further improvement of tax incentives for corporate (as distinct from individual) giving is *not* now a high priority. Even as regards individual giving, the slow takeoff of payroll giving (GAYE) appeared to owe more to defects in its marketing than in its tax incentive. There was sometimes a vague and unbusinesslike attitude to tax-efficiency within the existing framework of incentives. The point for action is not so much the development of new tax incentives as sharpening awareness of those which already exist.

11. [p.xii] Matching grants have proved effective in the hands of government. of the Charities Aid Foundation, and for promoting employee involvement within individual companies, and their use and cost needs further consideration.

12. [pp.xiii] Our highest financial priority – and a very high one – is for finding comparatively modest amounts of 'money for marketing', that is for better resourcing, especially staffing, of the national promotional agencies. Though their resources have improved greatly in recent years, we have seen in case after case that they remain inadequate for the work to be done.

13. [pp.xiii-xv] Multiplicity of promotional agencies is inevitable if the advantages of specialisation and the division of labour are to be realised, but confuses companies unless the division of labour is clear and the way to the right agency is signposted. Informants stressed particularly that BitC should concentrate on its role as a general promotional agency

and source of information and leave specific activities to the appropriate specialist agency.

14. [p.xv-xvi] Companies need 'reasons' for contributing to the community, providing clear standards of judgement at a time when demands on companies are increasing and confusing, and this means more than illustrations of best practice. Theory is powerful, and a concerted effort is needed from business organisations and business schools to consolidate the theory and ideology of corporate giving and incorporate it into the main stream of management thinking and education.

15. [p.xvi-xvii] The government has made a major contribution to the development of corporate giving both directly and through creating an appropriate national climate. Many company informants, however, resented what they saw as a tendency by government to expect business to 'pick up the tab' for what are properly government's own responsibilities, and would like to see government define its responsibilities more clearly. There is also – though this is a more marginal point a case for the government to clarify companies' own role in the community by adding to the Companies Acts a General Purposes clause, to the effect that companies have a general power to act towards the community 'in as responsible a manner as would be expected from a responsible citizen in the like circumstances'.

Local promotion

16. [pp.xvii-xviii] Our case studies show how local promotional action has developed in recent years, though still with a shortfall in each of them between what companies might reasonably be asked to contribute to local problems and the actual contribution obtained.

17. [p.xviii-xix] Though local circumstances are too different to allow any general pattern to be prescribed for the organisation of promotional activities at local level, there can here as elsewhere be conventions of good practice, and national as well as local agencies have a role in promoting them.

18. [pp.xix-xx] Informal promotion, person to person and firm to firm, is ultimately the key to approaching companies at local as well as national level, but informality is not enough. It needs at local as at national level the backing of a structured and collective approach such as was notably lacking in Hillingdon, which may well be typical of other 'non-priority' parts of the country.

19. [pp.xx-xxi] Few informants in our local case studies could see the whole picture of problems and possibilities in their area. Assembly and diffusion of a comprehensive data base is important for planning and action: the appropriate agency to do this will vary from place to place, but national as well as local agencies have a role in ensuring that it is done. For the longer run we see a large potential in Common Purpose's community leadership programmes, designed to produce cadres of local leaders from both the private and the public sector who see the whole local picture, are familiar with each other's problems, and are used to working together.

20. [pp.xxi-xxii] While the institutions and structures of local promotion must and will vary from place to place, business and the voluntary sector need in every area strong focal organisations working in partnership with each other and with the public sector. In the absence of clear focussing and signposting company informants can and do find the proliferation of agencies bewildering. We have noted in our case studies weaknesses, differing from one city to another, in the organisation for the promotion of community involvement of business, of local or other public authorities, and especially of the voluntary sector. Existing focal voluntary associations such as Councils of Social Service are underresourced. We see for the longer run important possibilities in the development of endowed community foundations, to which CAF is giving special attention at the moment, and of trusts promoting 'federated giving'. We would like to see much more use in Britain of the model of federated giving developed in America by the United Way, as set out in the appendix to Paper VI.

21. [p.xxiii] Given the variety of local promotional agencies and the fact that no single pattern can or should be prescribed, developing local promotion is a matter not of direction but of 'catalysing' action and cooperation – networking – among many different agencies. 'Catalysts' may be individuals or institutions, and do not come from any single source. We emphasise their role and the need to seek them out.

22. [p.xxiii-xxiv] 'Money for marketing' is if anything more important for local than for national promotion. We have found one local agency after another which is underresourced, and the addition of even one or two extra staff, full- or part-time, could make all the difference to the agency's ability to find time for the slow and laborious process of getting through to companies and for planning ahead.

Learning from America

23. [pp.xxiv-xxvi] America is 'different' only in the sense that the culture of corporate giving has been marketed there to companies for longer. It has taken a long time to develop, but with the encouraging finding that in the right conditions its development can be sharply accelerated, as it was in the 1980s for the same reasons as in Britain. There is no standard pattern of corporate giving in America any more than in Britain, but the level and efficiency of giving can be and have been raised by the same methods as are proving effective in Britain: a one to one, customised, often very personal approach to individual companies, backed with organised partnership and government action to provide the right general 'climate' and fiscal and legal arrangements. There are, however, the same warnings as in Britain that business priorities are the priorities of business and that business neither wishes to nor could take over the proper responsibilities of government: and that the practical effect of tax incentives on corporate giving may be less than is often supposed.

We have concentrated on American experience, as particularly relevant hitherto. European Community experience, however, will be increasingly relevant in the future, and we welcome the initiative of a group of companies and agencies which is preparing a report on company giving across the member states of the EC.

I What Companies Give and How They Give It

The total amount of company giving

> Would you bring in a lamp to put it under a tub or under the bed? Surely you will put it on the lamp-stand? (Mark 4.21)

In spite of the efforts of the Charities Aid Foundation and Directory of Social Change, the record of the non-commercial contributions of companies in Britain to the communities in which they operate remains a case as much of the tub as of the lampstand. Table 1 shows the most comprehensive available estimate, by Directory of Social Change: but it is certainly an underestimate, and even within its limits is imprecise.

Table 1   Estimated total community contributions by companies, 1988.

	£ million
Charitable donations	170
Sponsorship	42
Enterprise, training, education	30
Non-commercial advertising	20
Joint promotions	15
Secondments	8
TOTAL	285

Directory of Social Change, *Company Giving News*, November 1989.

No estimate could be made for the cost of gifts and provision of facilities in kind, though for some companies, depending on the nature of their product, gifts in kind are the largest item of all. The cost of secondments is

1

certainly underestimated: in a survey of 207 companies for the same year CAF found that the cost of secondments to them was upwards of £17 million. Besides formal secondments, a great deal of company staff time is made available in connection, for example, with school-business links or, at senior management level, with the formation and management of Training and Enterprise Councils (TECs), or by way of advisory services to enterprise or employment agencies; or, less commonly, through the release of work time for activities with voluntary organisations. The cost of these less formal releases of staff time is large, but cannot be estimated. Table 1 also excludes the cost of sports sponsorship (£182 million in 1988): because it is primarily a commercial activity, and yet it is not always or entirely so.

Table 1 also includes only what is contributed in the name of the company as such. Companies may and usually do encourage employee giving or volunteering: this is an important part of the corporate contribution, but its total value is not known. One item for which a figure can be given is tax-recoverable payroll giving under the Finance Act 1986, usually referred to as Give As You Earn, though strictly this is only one (though the most important) form of it. Though its start was slower than expected – this is dealt with in more detail in Paper II – within two years the annual value of contributions reached £6.5 million.

Nor does Table 1 include the consequences of past company giving. A donation towards endowment of a charity appears in the statistics of company giving in the year when it is made, but the later income from the endowment does not appear, even if the endowment is a transfer of capital otherwise available to earn revenue for the donor company, or if its form is such that the income on it still in fact comes out of the company's revenue. Wimpey's company reports, for example, record only modest annual charitable donations, but the Tudor Trust, endowed with thirty per cent of Wimpey's shares, is able to make grants of several million pounds a year.

Many of the data underlying even those items which are included in Table 1 are imprecise or incomplete. There will always be some degree of imprecision, since there is no clear line between what businesses do for commercial and non-commercial reasons. 'Enlightened self-interest', the key phrase in many businesses' community involvement today, has elements of both. But the chief reason for imprecision is that, wherever that line may be drawn, the statistics of what falls on the non-commercial side of it are imperfect.

The Inland Revenue should in principle be able at least to say, like the American Revenue, how much companies have given in tax-deductible or tax-recoverable form, but it cannot. It can, for example, give a figure for the total value of covenants to charities, but cannot break this down between company and other donors.

Companies, for their part, are required to declare 'exclusively charitable' money donations in their annual reports, but the declared figures are often far from including the full cost of what the Charities Aid Foundation defines as 'total corporate support' for non-commercial causes: in cash, kind, staff time (by way of formal secondments or otherwise), or arts or sports sponsorship. In surveys of 110 companies for 1987 and 207 for 1988 CAF found that the total cost of 'corporate support', so far as it was measurable, was two and a half to three times that of declared cash donations. But 'so far as it was measurable' was a large qualification, for companies themselves were often unable to say what the total cost of their giving was. In the 1989 edition of *Charity Trends* no estimate of 'total corporate support' could be given for half the Top 400 corporate donors, and the rest of the list was dotted with symbols showing that companies actually gave more support than was shown, but did not or could not quantify some of its elements. In our own 1990 survey of medium-sized companies there were too few valid replies to a question about the total cash value of contributions to make statistical analysis worth while. In one company we interviewed, the true figure for 'total corporate support' turned out, when the chairman assembled it specially for our visit, to exceed that of declared donations by a factor of around 100.

With all these reservations, however, it can be said at least that companies' non-commercial contributions are already a large resource for those who receive them: much larger than Table 1.1 by itself would indicate, and also more important than a superficial comparison with some other types of giving might suggest.

The total income of registered charities was £15 billion in 1985 and probably around £19 billion by 1988/9. Alongside this, £170 million of company charitable donations does not look much. It becomes more impressive, however, when it is seen as a contribution to one of the key elements in charities' resources, their 'voluntary' income from donations and fund-raising. An analysis by CAF for 1985 shows that 85 per cent of charities' income came from (in order of importance) fees, charges, and trading, government and other statutory grants, and investments. This left only 15 per cent, in that year under £2 billion, to come from 'voluntary' contributions. 'Voluntary' income is vital to charities for maintaining their voluntary and charitable character and giving them a margin for development: and companies' contribution to it, though still modest, is much more significant than a comparison with charities' total income would suggest.

Companies' 'corporate support' also, of course, reaches many parts which ordinary charitable giving does not, as with sponsorships, support for enterprise and employment agencies, or secondments or other release of staff time.

Moreover, corporate giving has grown while some other important forms of giving have stagnated. A comparison with charities' 'voluntary' income is again revealing. From 1975 to 1985 charities' income from all sources rose in real terms by 90 per cent, but their 'voluntary' income from donations and fund-raising by only two per cent. A sharp fall from 1975 to 1980 was followed by a strong recovery in 1980-85, but the most recent data point to a return to stagnation. By contrast, declared donations by the Top 200 company donors doubled in real terms from 1977 to 1986, followed by a further real increase to 1987, and another of nearly 20 per cent from 1987 to 1988. Per head of their work force, donations by the Top 200 almost trebled in real terms from 1977 to 1986. The percentage of pre-tax profits which they gave did not rise in the same way: the average in the 1980s was just over 0.2 per cent, up only slightly from 0.17 per cent in 1977/8. But the total profits of the Top 200 increased in real terms by 57 per cent from 1977 to 1986, so that donation of a fairly steady percentage yielded an increasing absolute amount.

To what do companies give?

CAF's survey of 207 companies, imperfect as its information was, gives a more detailed view than Table 1 of where company giving actually goes. Table 2 shows the overall pattern and Table 3 the destination of as much of the cash donations – 45 per cent – as could be assigned to particular causes. Donations to medical and health organisations stand out at the head of the list. The other big blocks are grants for 'community improvement', to organisations engaged in building and strengthening local communities; for education and 'general' research (grants for specialised research, as in health, were classified under the appropriate specialised head); for the arts; and for personal social service and other 'general welfare'. These five heads accounted for 76 per cent of identified donations, and most companies reported donations under each of them. 16.5 per cent of identified donations were spread over eight other heads, most of them (the exceptions are youth work and heritage/environment) supported by only a minority of companies: with a final 7 per cent going to 'other' organisations, including general grant-giving bodies and organisations concerned with 'promotion and advocacy of voluntary action'.

Table 2   Total 'community involvement', 207 companies, 1988

	Number of companies		
	indicating support	gave a cash value	Cash amount (£000)
Cash donations	202	177	61,085
Gifts in kind/facilities	95	39	4,131
Sponsorship	120	73	18,434
Joint promotions	34	6	567
Secondment	64	49	17,230
Enterprise agencies	83	42	3,982
Employment schemes	82	20	1,883
Other specified	84	24	8,282
Unassigned			26,400

Charity Trends, 12th edition.

Table 3   Destination of 'cash donations' in Table 2

			No. of organisations supported	
	Percentage to each destination	Percentage of companies supporting	Total	Max. no for any company
Medicine/health	22.7	72	2,881	425
Community improvement	14.9	60	417	76
Education/research	13.5	70	1,084	94
Arts	12.7	64	630	55
'General welfare'	12.4	67	1,526	201
Heritage/environment	5.4	61	474	98
Employment	4.1	39	186	40
International aid	2.6	33	170	30
Youth	2.1	62	377	44
Religion	1.0	26	179	30
Leisure	0.7	42	197	25
Animals	0.5	26	87	14
Housing	0.2	30	167	49
Other	7.1	41	592	71

Charity Trends, 12th edition. 'Percentage to each destination' is based on the 45 per cent of donations which could be specifically assigned.

Altogether, 8,967 voluntary organisations were identified as receiving donations, with some duplication but also some omissions. Note also, from the next column, that in extreme cases one company might be supporting anything from a dozen to over four hundred organisations under each head. 'Where so many organisations were supported', as CAF comments, 'it was the case that a little money was spread amongst a large number'. Looking at the table as a whole, especially at its bottom end, it is clear that the butter was often spread very thin.

Table 4   100 companies: percentage which do not normally support certain types of appeal

percentages

Local appeals not in areas of company presence	85
Purely denominational appeals	78
Circular appeals	73
Advertising in charity brochures	73
Appeals from individuals	71
Overseas projects	66
Large national appeals	53
Fund raising events	48
Other stated exclusions	4

Michael Norton, *Raising Money from Industry*, Directory of Social Change, 1989.

Directory of Social Change, from a questionnaire to 100 companies, turns the question of destinations the other way round (Table 4). To what do companies tend not to give? In none of the categories in the table is company support altogether excluded, but appeals which are too generalised (circular appeals, large national appeals), or purely personal, or unrelated to areas where a company operates may not get much of a hearing: nor may purely religious appeals, though this does not exclude appeals by social service organisations which have a religious basis. Our own interviews confirm that companies often have their doubts about the value of advertising in charity brochures and may reject 'glossy' appeals: more likely, as some see it, to benefit the printers than the cause.

Other common exclusions can be added to those in the table. A minority of companies make donations to political parties, but appeals which are either overtly political or have a political slant are usually not accepted. Though grants for health and education do in fact make up a large part of company giving, we were told repeatedly that companies resent being expected to 'pick up the tab' for basic provision which they see as properly the responsibility of government: the same point was sometimes made about personal social services and the arts.

There is no standard pattern of giving

What cannot be said, however, is that there is any standard pattern of company giving. Totals and averages are interesting, but once one comes down to individual companies the picture is one of immense diversity. As part of this study we re-analysed EXTEL data on declared charitable donations by companies of all sizes. The imperfections of these data mean that elaborate analysis would be pointless, but even a crude analysis brings out that, whether companies are compared by the size of their work force, by the volume of their pre-tax profits, or by the sectors in which they operate, average figures for what they give derive from a very wide scatter indeed.

Measuring first of all by size in terms of employment (Tables 5 and 6), it is broadly true, as might be expected, that the biggest companies make the biggest donations, but in every size band there are companies which declare large donations and others which declare very little. Most companies in all size bands declare donations in the range from 0.01 to 0.49 per cent of pre-tax profits, but again there is a wide scatter in each size band, though with one systematic difference: smaller companies tend to give more. In the size band 1-499, 25 per cent of companies gave 0.5 per cent or more: we have met one which is committed to donating 10 per cent, on the principle that a serious donations policy should be 'big enough to hurt'. In the band from 500 to 2999 the proportion giving at least 0.5 per cent fell to 16 per cent, and in companies employing upwards of 10,000 it was 7 per cent.

CAF gives a dramatic illustration of the range of giving between companies, whether large or small, from an analysis of declared donations per employee. In 1986/7 its Top 400 donors gave an average of £15 per employee, but the top twenty in terms of donations per employee gave between £267 and £867, and in two outstanding cases £1,275 and £2,333. One reason might be that some companies have large turnover and profits but few employees, but the top twenty also included companies with a substantial work force.

Measuring by the absolute amount of pre-tax profits (Table 7), it is again broadly true that the biggest donations are associated with the biggest profits, but once more with a wide scatter among companies with a given amount of profit.

7

Table 5 Total donations by company size (percentage of companies in sample by size band)

			No. of employees				
Donations	Base	1-499	500-999	1000-1999	2000-2999	3000-9999	10K+
£5000	371	34.5	24.5	24.0	9.2	7.0	0.5
£5000-9999	219	24.7	17.8	25.6	14.6	16.4	0.9
£10000-19999	170	16.5	14.1	29.4	14.7	18.8	6.5
£20000-49999	178	17.4	9.0	19.1	12.9	30.3	11.2
£50000-99999	81	8.6	3.7	14.8	8.6	45.6	18.5
£100000-499999	136	4.4	5.1	8.1	3.7	19.1	59.6
£500000-999999	22	4.5	0	9.1	0	18.1	68.2
£1 Million+	12	0	0	8.3	0	8.3	83.3
DK	1						
Total	1189	255	180	255	126	216	156

Source: derived from data supplied by EXTEL.

Table 6 Donations as percentage of profit by size (no. of companies)

			Donations, per cent				
Size bands	Base	0.01	0.01-0.09	0.1-0.19	0.2-0.49	0.5-0.99	1.0 1.99	2+
1-499	255	2	67	57	66	32	10	21
500-999	180	1	66	43	36	14	11	9
1000-1999	255	2	100	60	52	24	12	5
2000-2999	126	0	55	34	22	10	4	1
3000-9999	216	7	90	57	36	19	4	3
10000+	156	3	61	47	34	7	.4	0
DK	1	0	1	0	0	0	0	0
Total	1189	15	440	298	246	106	45	39

Source: derived from data supplied by EXTEL.

Table 7   Donations by profit level (no. of companies)

Donations	Base	Pretax profits (m)					
		<£1m	1-10	10-20	20-50	50-100	100+
£s							
<5000	371	61	264	31	11	3	1
5000-10000	219	13	145	47	13	1	0
10000-20000	170	10	86	44	19	9	2
20000-50000	178	3	57	42	56	12	8
50000-100000	81	0	16	12	23	19	11
100000-500000	136	1	10	10	20	25	70
500000-£1m	22	0	1	0	2	3	16
£1m+	12	0	0	0	0	0	12
Total	1189	88	579	186	144	72	120

Source: derived from data supplied by EXTEL.

CAF has shown that year to year changes in pre-tax profits tend to be associated with corresponding changes in donations, and the Finance Acts of 1986 and 1990 may have made this link stronger by allowing companies to make single tax-deductible donations, which can be changed from year to year, instead of committing themselves to a covenant over several years. But in individual companies profits and donations do not necessarily move together. Directory of Social Change, in an analysis of company reports for 1988/9, found a number of cases where companies had either increased their profits but reduced their declared donations or increased their donations in spite of reduced profits. Capital Radio's profits were up by 62 per cent but its donations down by 49 per cent: McCarthy and Stone's donations were up by 44 per cent in spite of a 79 per cent fall in profits.

The wide scatter appears again when companies are listed by the main sectors in which they operate (Table 8). Companies in the distribution and services sectors are somewhat more likely to declare donations equivalent to at least 0.5 per cent of pre-tax profits – they were 36.5 per cent of the companies in the sample, but 49 per cent of those giving 0.5 per cent or more – but even in their case the scatter is wide.

The extent to which companies invest in their communities in ways other than cash donations also varies widely. Half the companies in CAF's 1987 survey reported the cost of their 'total community involvement' as less than 1.5 times that of cash donations alone, but nearly two-fifths reported ratios

Table 8   Donations as percentage of pretax profit by sector (no. of companies)

Sector	Base	0.01	0.01-0.09	0.1-0.19	0.2-0.49	0.5-0.99	1-1.99	2+
				Donations per cent				
Agriculture	3	0	2	1	0	0	0	0
Energy/water	33	4	21	5	3	0	0	0
Metals/chem.	130	2	54	25	29	8	5	7
Eng./vehicles	242	2	102	70	39	18	6	5
Other manuf.	260	2	83	80	56	25	8	6
Construction	84	1	40	23	11	3	3	3
Distribution	187	3	55	44	50	24	4	7
Transport & comms	36	0	15	5	9	3	3	1
Bus. services	173	1	54	41	44	21	8	4
Other services	38	0	13	3	4	4	8	6
Not known	3	0	1	1	1	0	0	0
Total	1189	15	440	298	246	106	45	39

Source: derived from data supplied by EXTEL.

of at least two to one, and thirteen of these had ratios of over four to one: in the two extreme cases, Reed International and British Telecom, fifteen to one.

There are signs that the scatter of company donations may be narrowing. CAF's analysis of declared donations by the 400 biggest donors in 1986/7 showed a very sharp difference between the Top 50 and the rest. One reason why the Top 50 made relatively large donations was that they were on the average larger than the other 350, but another was that they gave at, by British standards, a high rate: on the average, 0.265 per cent of declared profits, and £24 per employee. The rest of the Top 400 gave £7 to £10 per employee – the last fifty gave only £3, less than the £4.30 which CAF found to be the median for a general sample of firms employing under 100 – and 0.1 to 0.16 per cent of pre-tax profits. More recent analysis by Directory of Social Change shows, however, that whereas giving by the Top 50 has tended to plateau in real terms, companies in the second and third hundreds have increased their declared donations by considerably more than the rate of inflation.

Nevertheless, the scatter remains wide and the pattern of giving unstandardised, and that leads on to a central question. Companies' circumstances and interests are different. They operate in different product and labour markets and different types of community. They are at different stages of development: established and stable, for example, or struggling with problems of start-up and growth. Their interests in community involvement and potential for it differ accordingly: one would not in any case expect either a uniform overall level of giving or a similar balance in every firm between giving in cash and kind, between support for charitable causes and enterprise or employment agencies, or between donations and sponsorship. But how far do differences in patterns of giving actually arise from rational consideration of factors like these – or are they more casual, reflecting accidental or personal circumstances and the absence of reasoned policies?

The contributions policies of medium-sized companies: survey results

To help towards answering this question, we sent a postal questionnaire to a sample from EXTEL data of 300 medium-sized companies, employing from 500 to 2,999, about their reasons for contributing to the community, the contents of their contribution programmes, and the way in which they manage them. 120 valid replies were received, with some bias towards the more generous givers, but otherwise well spread by size, sector, and ownership. We supplemented the survey results with interviews with thirty companies.

Why do they give?

By far the most strongly stressed reason for giving and community involvement (Table A1) was 'social responsibility – need to put something back into the community'. Second came 'personal views of the chairman or chief executive', and then, about equally, 'influence from employees' and 'enlightened self-interest – promoting the company's image'. 'Family tradition of the owners' was at least 'quite' important for one third of respondents. 'Influence from other firms' and 'tax incentives' registered low on the list.

Interviews put meat on these bones. 'Social responsibility' and the case for 'putting something back into the community' were stressed repeatedly. Sometimes this was in very general terms: 'a sense of duty' (toolmakers): 'we are not crass money-makers' (measuring equipment): 'it's human – a company is like an individual, only bigger' (communications equipment) – or, as the same firm added, 'everyone does it – everyone likes to feel good'. More specifically, companies recognised the different balance between 'social responsibility' and 'enlightened self-interest' in activities like charitable giving and in others more commercially-oriented, like sponsorship or promotional gifts of product: though elements of both were likely to be present in either case. Several companies made the point that charity, unlike sponsorship, is an area for 'playing it cool' rather than 'banging the drum'. We found in our approach for pilot interviews with a small random sample of companies that those with low levels of declared donations were most likely to refuse: but so did one with a high level whose policy was not to publicise what it gave.

Nevertheless, the line between 'social responsibility' and 'enlightened self-interest' was usually blurred. Declared motives ranged from 'sense of duty' (above) to, from another firm in the same city, 'I only do it for payback', but 'enlightened self-interest' usually came in alongside 'social responsibility'. In two television companies support for the community was seen as 'expected' in two different senses: because this was a condition of their franchise – it was claimed that at least one television company had lost its franchise partly because of failure under this head – and because, since television is a high-profile business reaching into every home, 'people expect to see us around'. Other high-profile businesses echoed the latter point: as one said, 'we and the community are interdependent'. An insurance company said that we used to be modest about our donations, but are now more aware of the importance of our image and are reshaping our policy accordingly. Companies which did not have the same high street or final consumer profile nevertheless followed the same line of thought. One reason why the toolmakers quoted above emphasised 'sense of duty' was doubt whether a publicised donations policy would actually make much impact on their particular customers. Another which produces basic raw materials for industry was still very much aware that its production process has nuisance value, and had argued at length with its parent corporation for a modest budget to establish its credentials as a good neighbour.

There could be same mix of motives where giving was seen as affecting recruitment and employment. An electronics company said that social responsibility 'drives' its community programme, but then illustrated how its programme varies from establishment to establishment according to its need to establish its status as an employer and the impact a community support programme could be expected to have for this purpose in communities of different kinds. Secondments were seen as a public service, but also as a way of easing out managers at the end of their careers or, more rarely, of mid-career development. School-business links were likely to be initiated by schools primarily for their pupils' benefit, with a response from companies at least partly on grounds of public service, but companies could also give a variety of reasons, including increasing problems of recruitment, why there was 'something in it for us'.

Even companies which underlined the distinction between altruistic and commercial giving recognised that altruism could and did have a payback in general public relations, and sometimes even more in employee relations. A cleaning materials firm with a high ratio of donations to pre-tax profits kept in principle a low profile in its donations, but the connection between its support for environmental causes and its deliberately 'green' image was not accidental. The point about employee relations could be rather general ('nice to support the place you live in' or 'a friendly place to work in'), but was also in a number of companies more specifically related to recruitment or to internal relations, particularly where employees themselves were directly involved. We were told several times that employee involvement not only generates interest, money, and voluntary effort but has a payback to the company through extending experience, developing skills, and pulling otherwise isolated staff together: 'people meet who would never meet otherwise'.

In some companies the factors of 'family tradition' or 'personal views of the chairman or chief executive' came through strongly, at least as a starting point. Some of the highest ratios of donations to profits which we met arose in this way: from the concern of the chief executive for social responsibility (property development), the decision and tradition of the family which owns the American parent company (the cleaning materials firm just mentioned), or the close link between family and community in a firm making a highly traditional product in small communities where it is a major employer. There is obviously a question whether these companies' practice would change if there were a change at the top, but the comment in each of them was that, for the time being at least, the practice of generous donations has been institutionalised: as part of the company or community culture, and in one case through the creation of a trust which holds 45 per cent of the company's shares.

How much do they give?

Tables A2 and A3 show the amounts which these medium-sized companies gave, in absolute terms and as a percentage of pre-tax profits. The proportion giving 0.5 per cent or more, 30 per cent, is well above the 16 per cent shown for the same size band in Table 6, probably indicating that our respondents were biased towards the more generous givers: though this is not certain, since our questionnaire asked for information on items which may not have been fully included in the declared donations on which Table 6 is based.

Two-thirds of these companies (Table A4) had increased their level of giving over the last three years, and two out of five expected to increase it over the next three years, compared to 11 per cent who foresaw a reduction. When, however, they were asked to name the maximum percentage of pre-tax profits which the company was likely to give, their answers (Table A5) corresponded rather closely to the percentage which they were giving already: if anything, it was rather lower.

That is not surprising, for interviews showed that budgets for charitable giving (sponsorship budgets are another matter) do in fact tend to grow incrementally – 'last year's figure plus inflation' – from some base established in the past: perhaps deliberately, by the board or the family, but often in less formal ways beyond informants' memory, and in either case not necessarily reconsidered as time went on. We quote in our Swindon study the example of no less a firm than Allied Dunbar, which in the early 1970s decided on an an absolute figure judged at the time to be adequate for a serious and substantial programme of giving: this happened to be about one per cent of pre-tax profits, and at one per cent, with a small addition for support to staff charities, the figure has ever since remained. We met one company which did find it necessary to reconsider an early formal decision. It decided early in the 1980s that its charitable budget should be £100,000 plus 15 per cent of distributed dividends: but then profits and dividends rose strongly, and at the end of the decade the company decided that the budget must be capped.

Historical accident, however, was the keynote where the total size of the budget was concerned, and one manager made a central point: whereas, he said, in other areas there is usually a rule of thumb, 'a percentage of something or other', by which to judge a budget, in the case of charitable giving there is not. We had several comments on the usefulness of the Per Cent Club, of which 18 per cent of respondent companies are members, in providing a standard which companies could 'latch on to'.

We asked companies (Table A6) which factors might restrict their overall level of charitable giving and community involvement in future. By far the most strongly stressed factor, and the only one mentioned as 'very important' by more than a small minority of companies, was 'financial position of the firm'. 93 per cent of those companies which gave a definite answer thought that this was at least 'quite' and 60 per cent that it was 'very' important. In every other case a majority of the companies giving a definite answer thought that the possible restrictions tabulated were 'not' important.

Nearly half, however, thought that 'lack of information on charities' might be 'quite' or even 'very' important. More than 40 per cent thought that opposition from shareholders might be at least a 'quite' important restriction or that there might not be enough tax incentives, and 30-35 per cent that there might be some restriction through lack of information about tax incentives, opposition from parent groups, or lack of interest on the part of employees. Comments in interviews, however, qualified these findings, chiefly in the direction of playing down the actual significance of these hypothetical restrictive factors.

'Financial position of the company' was mentioned chiefly with reference to crisis or possible crisis situations: not important, as one company said, 'unless we were going down the tubes'. The overseas parent of another company had experienced a major disaster, and this had led to a squeeze on, among others, community contribution budgets down the line.

Shareholder opposition also figured as a hypothetical rather than an actual restriction. We received very few comments about either positive or negative attitudes on the part of shareholders: community relations staff in one company commented that the problem for them was simply to persuade their board to keep the shareholders informed. A survey of institutional shareholders for CAF in 1985[1] found fairly clear-cut views about the direction and management of company giving. More attention should be given to business-related as distinct from purely charitable causes: 'hard to convert into effective PR', and institutional respondents, unlike our companies, tended to put public relations first as a reason for giving. Contributions programmes, they argued, should be steady, well-focussed, and related to companies' general business strategy. But when they were asked about the overall level of giving at which they might be worried about the diversion of money from shareholders, they tended to name percentages of pre-tax profits well above the average even for CAF's Top 50. None could remember a case where his institution had actually experienced concern over excessive giving, and the majority thought that companies could and should give more than they do. When presented with case studies from company reports, only a minority thought that a company with falling profits and a high ratio (2.4 per cent) of declared donations to pre-tax profits should therefore reduce its donations. It was clear in any case that this was an area about which many respondents had not seen reason to keep

1   Allied Research International, *The Views of Shareholders on Donations by Companies to Charity*, report to the Charities Aid Foundation, 1985.

themselves well informed. There are, as one of the managers whom we interviewed said, advantages in insignificance.

In one of our own interviews a director of a major shareholding institution confirmed the CAF findings. His institution might be worried about 'eccentric' giving (CAF respondents said the same) but, as regards the overall level of giving, the percentage of pre-tax profits at which he thought that the institution 'might start to wonder' was, allowing for imprecision in the statistics, at least five times the average for CAF's Top 50 and ten to fifteen times the average for the rest of its Top 400. Like CAF's respondents, he could not actually remember a case where his institution had been 'sufficiently provoked' to wonder.

Tax incentives were again a case of a hypothetical restriction dissolving when companies were asked about their actual experience. The fuller analysis in Paper II shows that, while improvements are possible and would be welcomed, these refer particularly to incentives for individual (including payroll) giving. So far as giving by companies as such is concerned, comments by our respondents showed that this is not a major issue.

'Lack of employee interest', again, might be translated in the light of our company interviews as 'failure to mobilise employees' interest' or to find suitable channels for it. There are certainly forms of giving in which it has at least hitherto been difficult to interest employees, in particular payroll giving (GAYE) under the Finance Act of 1986. Our prize example is the firm where the public relations manager assured us that GAYE was in operation, but on ringing up the relevant department found that he was the only subscriber. There are other areas of employee contribution, like organised volunteering from the workplace, where few companies have made much effort hitherto. But the clear impression from our interviews is that where companies make a serious effort to back employees' own fund-raising efforts or volunteering, or to involve them directly in managing the company's own contribution programmes, there is plenty of employee interest to be found and a variety of incidental paybacks to the company itself. We can quote companies where even GAYE is being brought to a respectable level of support.

One 'restriction', however, which did stand out in our interviews was 'lack of information on charities': how to deal efficiently with the rising tide of appeals from organisations of which companies may know very little. There are two sides to this. One is the efficiency of companies' own arrangements for managing their own contribution programmes and monitoring their results: we deal with this below. The other is the effectiveness of the voluntary sector itself in organising the flow of information to companies and creating intermediaries through which contributions especially from smaller companies, with limited staffs, can be channelled to voluntary organisations with efficiency in investigating original applications and in monitoring results. We take this up both in Paper II, on the agencies for promoting corporate giving, and in the case studies in Papers III-V.

What medium-sized companies give

The pattern of what these companies actually give (Table A7) corresponds to what might be expected from other sources. Nearly all make cash donations, two-fifths make gifts of equipment, and more than half are involved in sponsorships, but only 25-30 per cent support enterprise or training agencies, and only one in twenty make secondments. We were reminded several times that staffs have been slimmed down and in this size-band of companies are not in any case large, so that long-term secondments for mid-career managers are difficult. There is reason to think that ARC's new policy of promoting short-term and part time secondments may help here. The variety of patterns noted above from general statistics emerged again in interviews: variety both in the direction of giving and in its form: for one company, for example, by far the largest form of contribution was boxes of the company's product.

31 per cent of the sampled companies operate GAYE, on the face of it an impressive figure, but very much qualified, as is shown in later papers, by comments in our interviews about actual take-up. Even where a real effort at promotion has been made, the percentage take-up had rarely reached double figures. The fact that 22.5 per cent of companies make matching grants may be of more immediate importance. Our interviews showed that collective involvement of employees, in one-off fund raising events or a permanent employee charity – our Swindon case study has examples of how good practice in this respect can spread from company to company along local networks – is more likely than 'boring' GAYE to attract employees' enthusiasm, and matching company grants are an encouragement to this and an expression of company appreciation and support.

Efficient management?

The key question, however, looking back to the central issue raised above, is about companies' management of their contribution programmes. Granted that they face different situations and may have a variety of interests and motivations, are their programmes managed in a business-like way, well geared to their actual situations and potential?

The great majority – nearly 70 per cent – do not have 'a formal written policy on charitable giving and community activities' (Table A8). Very few (7.5 per cent – Table A9) have staff working full time on 'charitable donations policy/community involvement': in most companies this is managed part-time, which presumably also is also the case in the 30 per cent of companies that said that they had no staff engaged on it at all – if action is taken, after all, someone must be taking it, even if not full time. These figures would not, however, given the form of the question, include staff in marketing or public relations departments dealing with sponsorships.

In deciding where and how to make donations (Table A10), nearly all these companies rely on applications from charitable bodies, and most also take account of suggestions from employees. The proportion who mentioned information from CAF or from 'business organisations' (Table A11) was one in four in each case. 18 per cent were members of the Per Cent Club and 13 per cent of BitC, and 8 per cent supported ABSA. Practically none, however, used Directory of Social Change's *Corporate Donor's Guide* or the Council for Charitable Support's *Guidelines for Company Giving*, and very few reported that suggestions had come from shareholders.

Answers to a question about where decisions about giving were made (Table A12) were a mixed bag. The most common answers were 'chairman or chief executive' or 'a special committee', followed at a distance by 'local management': few companies referred to any formal 'employee-management group'.

Interviews, again, put meat on these bones. Our interviews covered a wide range of situations. At one end was a company with clear overall policies, a well-staffed community relations department, and a programme not only large but planned and monitored with careful consideration of value for money both to receivers and to the company – focussed, for example, to ensure that gifts are actually substantial enough to make a difference – and regularly revised: with, in addition, strong and effective involvement of employees. At the other was a company, also substantial, on which our investigator's final comment is worth quoting in full.

> 'Vague' is the word which comes to mind. No sign of keen interest in the wider community of business givers, no great awareness of them, and no sign of a willingness to use the coming merger as an opportunity to re-think

policy on giving and take some new measures. Generally content to potter
on as before in a very unambitious and vaguely benevolent fashion.

We suspect that if companies' readiness to respond had not biased our
interviews towards more generous and coherent givers, we would have
found a notable proportion towards the latter end of this scale: as a manager
in one high-donating company said of what he saw in other medium and
small companies around him, 'very tatty'. As it was, the most typical
situation fell somewhere in between: competent administration in detail –
the company officers whom we interviewed knew what they were about –
guided by common sense, but lacking in the sharp edge needed to ensure
the best value for money for companies and those to whom they give.

One must be careful not to be bemused with formalities. 'Not having a
formal written policy', for example, or not having one regularly referred to
and updated, was clearly by no means the same thing as 'not having a
policy'. In one company the personnel manager mentioned that a policy
had been drafted in 1985, but could not lay hands on the file: nevertheless,
the company had in fact a considered and clearly directed strategy. The
company quoted above where the chairman had to assemble the elements
of its community investment *ad hoc* for our visit, and the cost of community
contributions exceeded declared donations by a factor of 100, most
certainly had policies, and well-directed ones. We were warned more than
once from the side of receivers that an over-rigid and over-centralised
policy could, and did, stand in the way of rapid response to local needs and
initiatives.

Nevertheless, it is worrying to find that 70 per cent of our sample
companies did not have a formal written policy or at any rate one which is
updated, specific and going beyond mere generalities. The company where
the elements of its contributions policy had to be assembled ad hoc has for
decades manufactured a traditional and relatively unchanging product for
a steady market, in small and stable communities with which managers are
strongly and personally identified. It describes itself with pride as in every
sense a family firm: 'the family is there to stay and they assume their
employees are too'. In these conditions osmosis could be expected to
operate, and clearly has done so: the factors relevant to community
involvement were present in managers' heads even without formally
writing them down. Most companies, however, do not operate in
circumstances as simple and stable as this. Companies' circumstances
change, and so, as the whole of this report shows, does the general approach
of businesses to community involvement. Ownership may change (see the
example above of not using the opportunity of a merger to re-think the

company's policies), and staff, especially managers, move in, out, and on. An updated policy document can provide not only a guide to current operations but a base-line against which the case for new departures can be measured. We talked to two companies which were in fact getting their act together after major changes, but there is reason to think that too many do not.

At the operating level, interviews again showed reason to worry. It is not surprising that nearly all companies reacted to appeals: the question was whether they were also proactive in the sense of researching the field, seeing where their donations could best be placed and what changes might be needed from time to time, and monitoring results. The impression from our medium-sized companies was mainly reactive, in the case not only of charitable donations but, for example, of school-business links, where the initiative was said to come principally from the schools.

One very obvious reason for this, in companies of this size, was limitations of staff time in the face of the rising tide of appeals. In this size band, in Britain as in America (Paper VI), administration of the contributions programme is likely to be part-time. As one company pointed out, we have only 25 management staff overall, and others pointed to the way in which their staff had been slimmed down in recent years. Part-time management is not necessarily damaging, provided, to pick up a part-time administrator's criticism of what she saw in other companies in her area, that responsibilities are clearly assigned. The main obstacle to efficient company giving, she said, is that 'too many companies don't have people employed to do this job' and 'appeals get bandied about': 'it needs to be a recognised job', even if part-time, and not simply 'taking people away from their ordinary duties'.

We interviewed one large company, above the medium size band, which recently abolished its community relations department and was now managing wide-ranging national and local programmes, at a cost approaching seven figures, as a part-time activity of its General Manager Personnel (plus contributions from marketing and other departments), and of local line managers: and nevertheless with considerable local impact, judging from our own local case study, and a national reputation for pioneering in several fields. A weakness, however, was that the previous community relations manager had been able to get out of his office and follow projects through: now, at least at the national level, this was no longer possible. A recurrent theme in other companies was that brought out in Table A6: difficulty, with the staff resources available, in getting together adequate information about the voluntary sector, or of monitoring the impact of any but the larger donations.

There are various means of overcoming the problems arising from limitations on staff time, and they were used, though patchily. One company regularly asked the local Council of Voluntary Service to advise on projects. Others used community trusts as intermediaries for their own giving, or supported them as a general service to help medium and small firms towards efficient giving: though it was said more than once that it was better to pass only a proportion of donations through trusts and to keep a direct relation of donor to receiver for the rest. Several companies had delegated charitable giving to their own trusts, in at least two cases with their own full-time staff, and in one with an impressively strong body of outside trustees.

'Reactivity', however, was not only due to shortage of staff time. The managers whom we interviewed might know their own budgets and administer them in a competent and common-sense way, but we often found vagueness about what a company's total contributions budget was and how all the elements in its community involvement added up. It is difficult, as was said to us by one promotional agency, to know what to do next unless you know what you are doing now. Some managers were vague about the tax efficiency of their donations ('we leave it to the accounts department'), though use was also made of the services of CAF or community trusts. We met companies which either did focus their donations so as to ensure that the amounts given would make a real impact or had recently decided to do so – 'giving up the shotgun approach' or, as another comment went, 'identifying centres of excellence' in their programmes – but also a number which did not. Many companies lack procedures for making the best use of secondments, or understanding of how secondments might contribute to mid-career development as well as to phasing out managers near the end of their careers. Policies on employee giving and volunteering and employee involvement in company giving ranged from institutionalised and highly organised to vague benevolence, perhaps supported with ad hoc and discretionary matching grants.

Some subsidiaries and branches of large national corporations appeared to have a good and flexible working relationship between national and local giving, but we also met cases where this relationship needed to be overhauled. The problem in one company was that local management was free to make donations in kind, but not when it was a case of cash. In another company donations policy had been left exclusively to local managers, out of their own profit margins, and a certain lack of generosity had resulted:

this was being tackled as part of a general reorganisation of the company. There is a warning, however, in the example quoted above of a company where centralised decisions, in this case at international level, had stood in the way of what seemed to us the justified assessment by local management of the budget needed to cope with locally obvious problems of public relations. In another large subsidiary of a company with well-established national contributions policies, and in good standing in the Per Cent Club, it was obvious that the company's national policies had simply not penetrated to the senior manager in charge of contributions policy at local level.

Perhaps the almost complete lack of awareness among our medium-sized companies of the *Guidelines* of the Council for Charitable Support or of Directory of Social Change's *Corporate Donor's Guide* is a comment on the efficiency with which these sources of guidance have been publicised. It is also, however, a comment on these companies' slowness to seek out sources which could guide their contributions policies to better effect.

Conclusion
We would not wish this paper to be taken as in any way a condemnation of what companies give and how they give it. They are giving a great deal, in a great many ways, and their donations have been increasing while some other forms of giving have not. We are impressed, as said above, with the competence and common sense of the administrators whom we interviewed. But it could be done better, and there is room for greater giving, in the great majority of companies, before running into barriers such as objection from major shareholders; who appear, in fact, to be much more in favour of company giving (though with qualifications about its direction) than some of our respondents thought. We have no great revelation to offer about how it might be done better, for our review leads to advice of the same sort as has been offered previously by others like Directory of Social Change and CCS, but we pick out a number of points which stand out in our own findings.

1.   Statistics
The defects of the statistics of company giving are important for three reasons.

First, unless national as well as individual company data are improved, business will not get the full credit for its community involvement. We appreciate the reasons why many companies prefer to 'play it cool' on their own charitable donations rather than give them a high public relations profile. But it is important for the credit of business and the market economy as a whole that it should be seen that market efficiency and social responsibility can and do go together and how much, and where and in what forms, companies do actually invest in their communities.

Secondly, example is important: and not only that of the biggest and most examplary companies, before whose expensive and highly organised performance, as we found in Swindon, more modest companies may draw back in alarm.

Thirdly, accurate and complete statistics are an important element in the efficiency of companies' own budgeting and contributions management. To repeat one of our favourite quotations, you cannot know what to do next unless you know what you are doing now.

The practical question is about the way forward, given the existing differences in the ways in which companies compile their statistics and the inevitable imprecision in the line between what is 'charitable' and what is commercial. A good beginning has been made through the efforts of CAF and the Per Cent Club to encourage companies to declare their contributions on a standard basis. We would like to see this lead as soon as possible to a voluntary code of practice endorsed by the main business and accountancy bodies, and eventually to more clear-cut rules about the declaration of donations under the Companies Acts, and thereafter to the provision by the Inland Revenue of statistics of companies' tax-deductible and tax-recoverable contributions broken down in line with the new Companies Acts rules.

2. Good citizenship and the bottom line

We appreciate the point made in the *Guidelines* of the Council for Charitable Support that charitable support should so far as possible be distinguished in company data from what is commercial or near-commercial. In practice, however, the motives of good citizenship and concern for the bottom line are nearly always combined. We see dangers in the accent laid by a number of respondents to CAF's survey of shareholding institutions on slanting company giving more towards payback, either to the individual business or to business as a whole, at the expense of charitable giving where payback may be less clear. That would be to underestimate the strength of companies' interest in 'social responsibility', as it has emerged in our own findings, as well as the importance of the 'social' needs to which charitable giving can contribute.

Nevertheless, the factor of 'something in it for us' is strong and general, and there is a double lesson here for applicants for company support.

First, applicants should not underestimate the force of the social responsibility motive or stress too exclusively the benefits of their projects to companies. But, secondly, if companies and the community are interdependent, as many companies see it, then not only agencies offering a service with immediate business value – arts sponsorship, for example, or secondments as a means of career development as well as a service to receivers – but also those concerned with community development and social provision are rendering companies a service. We have found welcome signs, on the side both of business and of community or social service agencies, of recognition that the philanthropic or 'gift' relationship between givers and receivers should be modified towards a quasi-contract for services rendered: partnership rather than charity.

3.   Companies' contribution policies are and must be individual – but within a framework of rising expectation

The lesson from America as well as Britain is that companies' circumstances and potential differ too much to allow any single pattern of giving to be prescribed, and this applies to the overall level of giving as well as to its direction. But it is also clear that the overall level of giving by companies in Britain arises to an important extent from historical accident and incremental growth: 'repeating last year's budget with an adjustment for inflation'. Moreover, there are too many vaguenesses in estimating payback to companies and practical difficulties in the way of determining optimum impact on receivers to allow precise and objective definition of what each company should give. As the old scholastic writers used to say of the Just Price, 'the arithmetic Just Price is known to God alone'.

There can nevertheless be a climate of expectation about the general level at which companies should give, and the level of expectation can be progressively raised: Paper VI shows how this happened in the United States. The case of the two television companies which saw the expectation of substantial community contributions as at least an informal condition for the grant and continuance of their franchises suggests one possibility. 'Contract compliance' in public service contracts has been out of favour under the present government, but could be given a new emphasis in future. The most general way forward, however, is certainly that of the Per Cent Club.

Individual companies can and do pioneer in new levels and forms of giving, often under family or personal influence, but may perhaps in the process, as in one or two of those which we interviewed, jump so far ahead as to be out of sight of the ordinary firm. What the Per Cent Club has been doing is to set for the overall level of giving a standard, admittedly arbitrary (something to 'latch on to') based on what a wide range of established and profitable companies have found practicable and advantageous. Allowing for imperfections in the statistics, its initial target of 0.5 per cent of pre-tax profits is very close to the actual level of giving by CAF's Top 50 donor companies. The intention from the start was to raise this overtime to at least one per cent, and the Club's 1990 meeting decided that the time had come to encourage giving at this level. 'In time', as the Council for Charitable Support says in its *Guidelines*, 'the conventions of good practice are likely to become more standard'. In the case of medium and smaller firms we have seen the Per Cent Club process working, notably in Sheffield, the location of the first regional Per Cent Club. The majority view of respondents to CAF's survey of shareholding institutions as recently as 1985 was that per cent giving would never take off in Britain, but it has done so. As a manager in another city said, 'ten years ago, if anyone had suggested committing half of one per cent, I would have said that they were bonkers'.

Use of a calculator on the data in Tables 6 and 7 is enough to show how much more would be raised for community involvement if more companies of substantial size and with substantial profits raised their level of declared donations to 0.5 per cent of pre-tax profits: or, allowing for deficiencies in declared donation statistics, if they raised their total community contributions to around one per cent. Our evidence shows that it is likely that most of them could do this without running into barriers such as shareholder opposition. There might even, as CAF's survey of institutions found, be more enthusiasm among shareholders for increased giving – if they were better informed – than some of the respondents to our own survey of medium-sized companies expected. In general, as has been shown, the restrictions on raising the level of giving hypothesised by some of our respondents turned out to be much less important when companies were interviewed about their actual experience.

4. *Giving contributions management a sharper edge*
We have noted from our evidence warnings about overemphasis on formal procedures and about overformalisation and overcentralisation. Contributions management can be effective, in some circumstances, without a formal policy or overall budgeting. Rigid headquarters control can leave too little flexibility to meet changing needs out in the field, or to meet them rapidly. Full-time management is not always essential: part-time

management can be effective, and the levels of staffing appropriate for large companies cannot reasonably be expected from smaller firms. But, having said this, we agree with the comment quoted earlier that contributions management in the medium and smaller companies with which we have been specially concerned is too often 'tatty'. Some of the points which still need attention, in spite of the competence in detail which we found among administrators whom we interviewed, are as follows:

- Formal, specific and regularly updated policy for contributions, supported with overall budgeting, may not always be essential but is certainly desirable, and it is worrying that 70 per cent of respondents among our medium sized companies do not have one;
- Responsibility for programme administration, even if part-time, needs to be clearly assigned and accounted for: 'a regular job', as one of our informants said, not simply 'taking people away from their regular duties', and backed with opportunities for training and for networking with experienced specialists;
- If company policies are to yield the best results either for companies themselves or for the causes which they support they need to be proactive: searching out and reviewing the most useful ways in which to place their support, where appropriate (especially in smaller firms) with the help of intermediaries: focussing their giving so as to have maximum effect, with full consideration of tax efficiency: and monitoring the results. Too often they are not.
- 'Reactivity' may reflect simply a company's lack of considered policies, but another reason is difficulty, especially for smaller companies, in committing enough staff time to do all that a proactive policy requires. That can be overcome in several ways, including delegation of giving to company trusts, seeking external advice, for example from Councils of Voluntary Service, and use of intermediaries such as community trusts for at least part of a company's giving. The intermediaries, however, must be there, and, whatever channels of giving a company uses, it has a right to expect that information about possible causes to support shall be readily and conveniently available, something more than the 'mountain of appeals'. We take up these points in Paper II.
- In a number of companies the balance and flow of information and influence between contributions management at headquarters and in subsidiaries or the field needs reconsideration: too tight control from the centre, or too little, or blocks in the channels between the two.

5. Carrying the message

In all this, we are saying little that is new. Guidelines bringing out points such as we have made are already available from CCS, Directory of Social Change, Business in the Community, or specialist organisations such as Action Resource Centre, the Community Projects Foundation, or the Council for Industry and Higher Education. The experience and documentation of a number of already well organised companies are available to be drawn on by others. There are research reports which provide a useful lead. The Institute for Manpower Studies, for example, reported in 1989 on *Stimulating Jobs: the Charitable Role of Companies*, bringing out policy implications for both companies and enterprise and employment agencies: these are conveniently summarised in an article in *Regional Studies*[2]. Theresa Crowley-Bainton and Michael White[3] have shown the payback to companies in a tightening labour market of targeting recruitment on the unemployed and ethnic minorities, primarily for commercial reasons but also from 'the desire to contribute to the local community and to social well-being': as clear a case as any of the advantages of enlightened self-interest. The Henley Centre's 1989 report on *Planning for Social Change* suggests a 'framework for corporate responsibility' and includes revealing analyses of how charitable giving may affect companies' corporate image and stimulate consumer response. One for Body Shop, for example, shows that its relatively high charitable donations and strong 'green' image give it only a moderate profile on the average among consumers of all classes, but a very high one among those in classes A and B who are in fact its principal market.

But the fact remains that there are many companies to which the message has not yet been effectively carried. As the Henley report says from its own findings, 'as in effect a marketing exercise in pursuit of enlightened self-interest, charitable activity is badly managed by most UK companies'. How, then, can the message be carried better to those companies which have not yet heard it? That is the subject of Paper II.

2   H. Metcalf, R. Pearson, and R. Martin, 'The Charitable Role of Companies in Job Creation', *Regional Studies*, June 1990.

3   Theresa Crowley-Bainton and Michael White, *Employing Unemployed People: How Employers Gain*, report to the Employment Service by the Policy Studies Institute, 1990.

Table A1   Importance of influencing factors (no. of companies, per cent of respondent sample (120) in brackets)

	Very		Quite		Not	
Enlightened self interest	14	(11.7)	65	(54.2)	31	(25.8)
Social responsibility	71	(59.2)	44	(36.7)	2	(1.7)
Family tradition of owners	13	(10.8)	27	(22.5)	58	(48.3)
Tax incentives	1	(0.8)	21	(17.5)	72	(60.0)
Views of chairman/md	26	(21.7)	50	(41.7)	29	(24.2)
Employees	12	(10.0)	61	(50.8)	32	(26.7)
Firms	1	(0.8)	13	(10.8)	77	(64.2)
Other (local dimension)	2	(1.7)	1	(0.8)	0	(0.0)
Not answered	27	(22.5)	8	(6.7)	23	(19.2)

Table A2   Spending on charitable giving (no. of companies, per cent of respondent sample (120) in brackets)

- Approx. amount in latest financial year

under £ 1000	- 1	(0.8)
1000-4999	- 19	(15.8)
5000-9999	- 21	(17.5)
10000-19999	- 24	(20.0)
20000-49999	- 30	(25.0)
50,000	- 25	(20.8)

Table A3   Approx. percentage of pretax profit donated (no. of companies, per cent of respondent sample (120) in brackets)

less than 0.5%	- 55	(45.8)
0.5-0.99	- 10	(8.3)
1-1.99	- 16	(13.3)
2 +	- 10	(8.3)
not answered/ negligible	- 29	(24.2)

Table A4   **Association with organisations promoting corporate giving (no. of companies, per cent of respondent sample (120) in brackets)**

Per Cent Club	-	22	(18.3)
Business in the Community	-	16	(13.3)
Action Resource Centre	-	4	(3.3)
Council for Charitable Support	-	0	(0.0)
ABSA	-	10	(8.3)
none of above	-	89	(74.2)

Table A5   **Maximum percentage of pretax profits likely to be given (no. of companies, per cent of respondent sample (120) in brackets)**

less than 0.1%	-	19	(15.8)
0.1-0.49	-	42	(35.0)
0.5 0.99	-	14	(11.7)
1 per cent	-	13	(10.8)
over 1 per cent	-	15	(12.5)
not answered	-	17	(14.2)

Table A6(a) Importance of potential constraining factors (no. of companies; percentage of respondent sample (120) in brackets)

	Very		Quite		Not	
not enough tax incentives	9	(7.5)	31	(25.8)	56	(46.7)
opposition from shareholders	11	(9.2)	30	(25.0)	49	(40.8)
opposition from parent group	13	(10.8)	12	(10.0)	53	(44.2)
lack of employee interest	5	(4.2)	27	(22.5)	60	(50.0)
lack of info. on charities	17	(14.2)	28	(23.3)	46	(38.3)
lack of info. on tax	8	(6.7)	21	(17.5)	62	(51.7)
financial position of firm	65	(54.2)	36	(30.0)	8	(6.7)
other	1	(0.8)	0		0	
(lack of clear benefit to company)						
not answered	42	(35.0)	37	(30.8)	31	(25.8)

Table A6(b) Importance of potential constraining factors (base = no. of companies answering by question; percentage of respondents by question in brackets)

	Very/Quite		Not	
not enough tax incentives	40	(41.7)	56	(58.3)
opposition from shareholders	41	(45.6)	49	(54.4)
opposition from parent group	25	(32.1)	53	(67.9)
lack of employee interest	32	(34.8)	60	(65.2)
lack of info. on charities	45	(49.5)	46	(50.5)
lack of info. on tax	29	(31.9)	62	(68.1)
financial position of firm	101	(92.7)	8	(7.3)

Table A7   Forms of giving (no. of companies; percentage of respondent sample (120) in brackets)

- Type of gift

cash donations	-	117	(97.5)
gifts of equipment	-	47	(39.2)
sponsorships	-	67	(55.8)
brochure adverts	-	60	(50.0)
use of facilities	-	23	(19.2)
secondments	-	6	(5.0)
other	-	15	(12.5)

  (CAF, covenants, gifts of products)

- Destination of donations and other gifts

charities/vol. bodies	-	117	(97.5)
schools	-	75	(62.5)
higher education	-	35	(29.2)
training agencies	-	25	(20.8)
arts/cultural bodies	-	62	(51.7)
enterprise agencies	-	34	(28.3)
other	-	11	(9.2)

  (hospitals, hospices, sports clubs, etc.)

- Company schemes

GAYE	-	37	(30.8)
company trust	-	23	(19.2)
covenant schemes	-	53	(44.2)
employee matching	-	27	(22.5)
other	-	8	(6.7)
(special events etc.)			
not answered	-	23	(19.2)

Table A8 Written formal policy on company donations/community involvement (no. of companies; percentage of respondent sample (120) in brackets)

Yes	- 35	(29.2)
No	- 83	(69.2)
not answered	- 2	(1.7)

Table A9 Number of firms with staff working on donations policy/admin. (no. of companies; percentage of respondent sample (120) in brackets)

firms with full time staff	- 9	(7.5)
firms with part time staff	- 77	(64.2)
firms with no staff assigned	- 36	(30.0)
not answered	- 1	(0.8)

Table A10 Information sources used by companies (no. of companies; percentage of respondent sample (120) in brackets)

applications from charities	- 114	(95.0)
employees	- 81	(67.5)
CAF	- 30	(25.0)
shareholders	- 6	(5.0)
business organisations	- 30	(25.0)
Guidelines for Co. Giving	- 1	(0.8)
Corporate Donor's Guide	- 1	(0.8)
other	- 4	(3.3)
(Community Trust, 'grassroots', CVS, trustees)		
not answered	- 3	(2.5)

Table A11   **Policy on levels of charitable giving (no. of companies; percentage of respondent sample (120) in brackets)**

- Level of giving over last 3 years

increased	-	82	(68.3)
stayed the same	-	35	(29.2)
decreased	-	3	(2.5)

- Plans to increase level of giving over next 3 years

yes	-	47	(39.2)
no	-	60	(50.0)
n/a	-	13	(10.8)

Table A12   **Source of decisions on donations policy (no. of companies; percentage of respondent sample (120) in brackets)**

chairman or chief executive	-	53	(44.2)
special committee	-	49	(40.8)
local management	-	30	(25.0)
employee/management group	-	9	(7.5)
other	-	16	(13.3)

(company secretary, board members, trustees, community relations managers)

II National Promotion of Company Involvement

National action to promote company involvement is not new. The Charities Aid Foundation, to use its current name, began its work of simplifying corporate giving and making it tax-efficient as soon as the Finance Act of 1922 made seven-year covenanting possible. The real take-off, however, was from the 1970s. Since then a new army of agencies has entered the field, and national promotion has risen in a great wave.

One reason was the unemployment, inner city decay, and general social turbulence of the 1970s and early 1980s: bad for business, as many business leaders saw it, and giving business a bad image. Companies, it was increasingly seen, had something to contribute to solving these problems in their own as well as the public interest.

A second reason was political change. Under Conservative governments since 1979 there has been a shift from action by the State to encouraging and enabling action by the private and voluntary sectors in a whole range of fields from education, training, and employment to social welfare, the arts, or the regeneration of cities and the environment. As a local government officer said to one of us in a study of London boroughs: my previous Labour authority saw a problem and asked 'What can we do about it?', but my present Conservative authority says 'What can we get done about it in the community?'. Business leaders responded to this change of emphasis. As the Institute of Directors said in 1987 in its report on *A New Agenda for Business*: if the aim is to create a genuine, stable, and enduring 'enterprise culture', then it is no longer enough for business leaders simply to mind their own business. The IOD rated 'helping to solve public problems' and 'contributing to public service competence' as objectives on a level with up-grading business leadership or improving industrial relations.

A third reason has been the American example. As Paper VI shows, there was from the end of the 1970s a new surge of company giving in the USA, encouraged as in Britain by political change and a new emphasis on action by the private and voluntary sectors. This led not only to an increase in the quantity of corporate community involvement but to a number of new departures. Some earlier features of American company giving, like federated giving through local United Ways, were not generally taken up in Britain, but in the changed British climate these newer departures attracted attention and imitation, often with direct support and encouragement from the USA.

The question today, therefore, is no longer whether something should be done at national level to promote company involvement. It is more a matter of observing the rising tide and seeing where among its swirling and sometimes confusing currents – after allowing, since we are dealing with a dynamic situation, for what is in any case likely to happen as current trends develop – something may still be missing, more effective use might be made of what is already being done, or confusion might be sorted out.

The areas in which the agencies of national promotion work are not always clearly demarcated. Agencies may have a finger in several pies, and any one pie is likely to have several fingers in it. The government's 1987 handbook on school-business links, *Industry Matters*, listed thirty-odd promotional agencies at national level alone. There can, therefore, be no neat classification, but, as a broad guide, the areas of promotional action and the agencies with a particular interest in each can be listed under four heads.

- General promotion of business involvement (Business in the Community).
- Specialised promotion: commitment to an overall level of giving (the Per Cent Clubs); secondment and volunteering from the workplace (Action Resource Centre, Volunteer Centre); arts and social sponsorship (ABSA and Action Match): employment of disdvantaged groups, environmental improvement (the Bridge Group); business-education links (the Foundation for Education Business Partnerships and the Council for Industry and Higher Education); federated and tax-efficient giving (Charities Aid Foundation).
- Information and integration: the information services of the Charities Aid Foundation and Directory of Social Change; community leadership programmes (Common Purpose); developing and promoting a general theory of business involvement in the community (the management schools).

• The government's input: finance; action agencies, including Training and Enterprise Councils; and general promotional support.

This paper is mainly descriptive, but issues emerge as the description goes on. There is no disagreement that marketing company community involvement requires a direct and tailor-made approach to the individual company and a person to person approach to key decision makers. All the usual techniques of marketing, however, can be and are being used to attract attention and open the door, and there are continuing issues about the way in which this is being or should be done.

General promotion of business involvement: business in the community (BitC).

BitC was set up in 1981, following a conference in 1980 between business and government representatives from Britain and the USA to consider how the private sector might help to solve problems in urban areas and be motivated to do so. It describes itself as:

> An association of major UK businesses committed to working in partnership with each other, with central and local government, voluntary organisations and trade unions to promote corporate social responsibility and revitalise economic life in local communities. BitC does this by working with its members and others to take action which demonstrates the creative role that business can play in economic revitalisation and enterprise, mainly through pioneering projects which can be replicated on a wider basis and through forms of business support which can become part of mainstream business practice.
>
> BitC, *Review of the Year 1988.*

The partnership extends, however, beyond business. BitC's members include government departments, the TUC, the main local authority associations, NCVO, and promotional organisations like Project Fullemploy or the Volunteer Centre. At the start it had twelve members, but growth has been continuous, to 119 members in 1985 and 445, including over half the top 200 companies of the Times 1000, by the autumn of 1989.

BitC services its own member companies directly, but works largely through promoting independent or cooperative activities with which other companies may be associated. It needs for this the influence and resources of large companies, but not necessarily a mass company membership of its own. Perhaps 500 companies, it was suggested in one interview, might be a reasonable target for BitC's own membership. The total number of companies involved in the activities which BitC supports and promotes is far greater. A good example is companies' involvement with enterprise agencies, which BitC promotes and services. It did not invent them, but their 'growth was slow', as the Institute of Manpower Studies' review of the agencies comments, 'until the founding of BitC'. There were 23 agencies in 1981 but nearly 400 by the end of 1988, most typically with 10-30 sponsoring companies, and by 1985 over 2,200 companies were involved in them. BitC's influence 'cascades down', as one comment put it, from the central core of members to this much wider circle.

Recruitment of companies to direct membership of BIC has normally been through a one-to-one approach: 'Steve or whoever' talks to the chief executive or community programme manager. Fine, it was said, for bringing in the companies at the top of the pyramid, but this method of recruitment is time and cost intensive. When in 1988 BitC's Marketing Business Action Team opened a campaign to increase community involvement among small and medium companies, it adopted a two-level approach. A campaign through direct mail and advertising was piloted in Humberside in 1989 and is being extended region by region in 1990, with the aim eventually of attracting around one thousand companies into new forms of involvement. The final approach is still through direct personal contact – response to mailshots leads on to contact and discussion with BitC's regional staff – but the opening gambit is different. The first results of the campaign indicate that the target of one thousand companies may well be reached.

The reasons why companies support BitC have changed. At the start, motivation owed a great deal to the depression and social unrest of the 1970s and early 1980s: unemployment, inner city riots, the gap, as some business leaders saw it, between business and the community, misunderstanding of the profit motive, industry's bad name, and the need to restore the image of the company as part of society. As the pressures of emergency receded, however, more positive motivation emerged. By 1988 BitC'S *Review of the Year* noted 'a substantial shift in emphasis over the past five years. Corporate responsibility is now demonstrated by action beyond philanthropy'. More companies are now contributing, as a BitC informant said, because they see support for the community not merely as an act of charity but as in their own continuing interest, in prosperity as in depression.

As BitC's support has grown, so has its budget. From £443,000 in 1984/5 it rose to £3,146,000 in 1988/9, not including support in kind, notionally valued for 1988/9 at £900,000, particularly support through secondments. For 1989-90 the division of expenditure was:

Programmes:	Per cent
Enterprise	16
Education-business partnerships	11
Other	10
Regional and other operations	28
Business leadership teams	8
Communications and public affairs	8
Member services	6
Administration & Chief Executive's office	13
	100

The range of BitC's promotional activities is very wide indeed. It houses and services the Per Cent Club. It promotes and supports local enterprise agencies and Youth Enterprise Centres, employment initiatives, education-business partnerships, and partnerships for town and neighbourhood development. A first 'one town' partnership was started at Halifax in 1986. This and initiatives by the CBI and the Phoenix Initiative led on to the promotion by the three agencies jointly, through Business in the Cities (now absorbed into BitC), of local business leadership teams in problem areas. By February 1990 there were eleven teams in place and another eight in process of formation or under discussion.

The emphasis of BitC's activities shifts as its programmes develop and the economic and social situations with which it has to deal change. The current range of its promotions is illustrated by the terms of reference of the eleven 'target teams' which it has set up since 1987.

- Enterprise development through enterprise and youth enterprise agencies.
- Finance for enterprise: private sector initiatives particularly for small and new enterprises, and including ethnic minority business development.
- Local purchasing: support by large for small businesses through purchasing and production and marketing assistance.
- Priority hiring: targeting employers' recruitment and training policies towards disadvantaged groups, particularly unemployed young people in inner cities.
- Education-business partnerships: promotion of school-based partnerships and of education compacts (40 by 1989) to improve performance and job opportunities for school leavers.
- Urban regeneration: promoting business involvement in job creation through property development, creation of work space, housing, and general improvement of the built environment.

- Voluntary sector initiatives: business involvement in voluntary sector initiatives for local economic regeneration. The team's 'flagship project' is promotion of employee community involvement (ECI), including volunteering from the workplace: aiming in the first place 'to persuade 100 of the UK's largest employers to undertake to create a climate in their companies which fosters ECI'.
- The Women's Economic Development Initiative, to promote women's enterprise and training.
- Business in the Environment, concerned with 'sustainable development through action and partnership between business and the community'.
- Rural enterprise. Much of BitC's activity has been concerned with urban areas, but by 1987 it was noting that 'there are serious problems emerging in rural areas comparable to those in inner city areas'. This led to a special conference for 100 enterprise agencies with a rural focus, a publication, *Work for the Countryside*, on how companies can help rural enterprise, and to the establishment of the target team.
- Marketing business action: demonstrating the value of community action to companies, with as a flagship project the mobilisation of small and medium companies for wider involvement in their communities, through the marketing campaign noted above.

This is a miscellaneous list of activities, in a wide variety of fields, and changing with changing circumstances. BitC's own contribution is often blurred because so much is done through other agencies which it promotes or supports, or through cooperation with local and national government, business groups like the CBI, and voluntary agencies such as those with which it is associated in the Bridge Group (below). Spheres of influence are often not clear-cut. BitC's activities and those of specialised promotional agencies overlap – that was a reason for creating the Bridge Group – and there is again an overlap between the roles of BitC and of general purpose business associations like the CBI, the Institute of Directors, or the British Institute of Management. These associations tend to leave the general promotion of company involvement to BitC. IOD and BIM have published reports on corporate social responsibility, but with little follow-up: a proposal for a similar CBI report was dropped. Nevertheless, all three associations overlap with BitC in promoting business-education links, and the joint launch of Business in the Cities originated in the CBI's work on *Initiatives Beyond Charity* and a first major CBI project in Newcastle.

It is not surprising that our own interviews with companies and local agencies show that out in the field BitC's image is often blurred, remote, and confusing. As one witness rhetorically exclaimed, BitC 'reorganises itself every six months'. BitC itself has been aware of its image problem, and at the end of 1989 launched the concept of a *New Look for the 1990s*. It had, it thought, tended to be identified with individual activities and projects rather than with 'its primary objective of promoting company involvement in all its facets'. Confusion had arisen because so many new agencies had entered the field since BitC began. A 'new corporate identity' was needed to 'clarify its position as the leading force in the UK in driving forward business involvement in the community'. Leading communications companies collaborated to develop a four-point strategy for BitC's 1989 AGM, including a short definition of objectives and target audiences, a new range of communications tools, a new corporate identity, and a new communications programme to be developed in 1990 and aimed at top business leaders, their likely successors, and mainstream as well as community affairs managers. The AGM also endorsed *Companies in the Community*, three pages of 'guidelines for company boards on how they can contribute to community regeneration through mainstream business activity'.

What a number of our informants see, however, is more than an image problem. BitC has indeed a clear role as 'the leading force in the UK in driving forward business involvement in the community', but what we have been told many times is that this needs to be more sharply demarcated from that of the specialised promotion agencies. BitC, as these informants see it, has a permanent and necessary role of four kinds: in attracting companies' attention to the opportunities and advantages of community investment, as it is doing through its Marketing Business Action campaign: as a forum for reviewing business involvement and 'promoting promoters' to fill gaps; as a central source of information about successes and failures in business involvement; and as a lobby for the whole complex of promotional agencies. But they would like to see BitC adopt more decidedly the philosophy of 'getting something done in the community' rather than acting directly itself, for they see it as duplicating what might be better done by specialised agencies and in the process both creating confusion and falling short in its general promotional role. Has BitC, one informant asked, put enough effort into documenting successful projects and supplying 'ammunition' for approaches to companies? And are there not areas like Hillingdon where problems may not be dramatic, but useful and unexploited opportunities for business leadership exist, and BitC might therefore take the lead in focussing and catalysing it as it has done through business leadership teams in a limited number of 'priority' areas?

Promotion in special fields
Promoting an overall commitment to corporate giving: the Per Cent Clubs

A national Per Cent Club of company chairmen and chief executives was launched by the Prince of Wales in December 1986, on the initiative of Sir Hector Laing and Sir Mark Weinberg, and on the model of Per Cent Clubs in the USA. Club members are committed to making community contributions in any form – cash, kind, secondments or other release of staff time, support for charities, the arts, Business in the Community, civic regeneration, or whatever – to the value of at least half of one per cent of pre-tax profits.

There had been scepticism about the idea of per cent giving. In 1985 a survey of major institutional shareholders for the Charities Aid Foundation found near-unanimity that this type of club would never take off in Britain. Respondents were not hostile to company giving: their consensus was that companies should if anything give more than they then did, and that their contributions were far from reaching a level at which the institutions might be worried lest too much was being diverted from shareholders' pockets. Per cent giving, however, was another matter. The institutions saw the UK as a highly taxed welfare state where charity is regarded as an extra, to be dispensed at companies' discretion. British managers were more individualistic, conservative, and resistant to outside pressures than those in the USA – less of a 'herd animal' – and less ready to treat charitable giving as a form of business promotion; and there was less chance in Britain than in America that shareholders would positively push for a generous contribution policy.

These informants, however, had misjudged the signs of the times: the national climate had changed. The Per Cent Club did in fact take off strongly, though its founders judged it wise to set the initial standard well below the minimum of two per cent expected in Per Cent Clubs in America, subject to raising it later if experience justified this. A move from the original standard of half of one per cent towards encouraging one per cent was made in 1990. 52 companies were members at the start. By the end of 1989 there were 250, including two out of five of the top 500 of the Times 1000 companies, and membership was growing at around 130 a year.

Many even substantial companies, as Paper I shows, do not reach the percentage target. Others, notably some of the major oil companies, still dislike the idea of joining a club. Some 'prefer to keep their light under a bushel'. Others again feel that they cannot commit themselves to a fixed percentage because their profits fluctuate: though the Club is in fact happy to relate the minimum commitment to a trend instead of to individual years, and most respondents in the survey of institutions just quoted did not think that a temporary downturn in profits need be reflected in a cut in contributions. Allowing for all this, it was thought in 1989 that membership among the top 500 companies might reach about 275.

Meantime, the second 500 were being 'worked on', and new developments aimed at medium and smaller companies were on the way. The Prime Minister, in giving strong personal support to the club at its 1988 AGM, in an address on *Companies Commmitted to the Community*, noted that the Prince of Wales had suggested a target of 500 members. Why not 600 or 700, including more small and medium companies? At the end of 1989 regional Per Cent Clubs aimed at local and smaller companies were started at Sheffield and Newcastle. The Sheffield club began with fifty members, and by March 1990 had 68, with an immediate target of 100 out of the 300 largest local employers. Further clubs are under consideration.

Recruitment to the clubs is by direct personal approach. In the national club this opens with a letter from the club's joint chairmen, followed by personal contacts and discussion: perhaps six to ten contacts might be needed per new member. The Sheffield club similarly works through members' personal contacts at top company level: ask members who they know in a company, it was said, supply them with literature, then 'you go and ask your friend Jack'. A tactful application of invidious comparison, it was also said, can help in 'Britain's biggest village', where managing directors do in fact watch what their competitors are doing. Localised recruitment is in any case easier because it is simpler for people to get together for a lunch and to make contacts with their friends.

The Per Cent Clubs have no formal constitution or activity, beyond an annual meeting. Business in the Community meets national running costs: the Sheffield Club's secretary is a volunteer. The point of membership, Sir Mark Weinberg said at the 1988 AGM, is threefold. 'By banding together and publicising our commitment to the community, we encourage other companies': in this way we also 'bring home to the community as a whole the fact that companies do care': and the contacts opened through the Club enable companies to learn from each other's experience. The charitable donations which companies formally declare under the Companies Act are often only a fraction of their total contributions to the community: since publicity and 'encouraging other companies' are important, the Club is now encouraging its members to produce full and classified accounts.

At local level, on the early experience of the Sheffield club, more specific activities may develop: organising publicity for members' community involvement (if they want it, which not all do), circulating a list of charities which receive and might receive donations, occasional joint fund-raising (£16,500 was raised at Sheffield's first annual dinner), perhaps setting up a holding fund to meet emergencies and smooth the flow of donations to receivers.

There are certainly unexploited possibilities in the Per Cent Clubs. Regional Per Cent Clubs have shown their potential for spreading the gospel of community investment to companies and levels of companies which national promotions do not reach: but there are still only two of them. Nationally and locally, there are many informal and personal links between the clubs and other business initiatives: there is a case for making these more specific and so sharpening the message which the clubs pass through to their members. Though the Per Cent Clubs are under BitC's umbrella, our impression is that companies are not always aware of how the clubs fit in with and contribute to BitC's mission. Should it not be a normal expectation, one informant asked, that Per Cent Club members should also be members of BitC? The message itself, of course, has to be available: the comment quoted above about a greater role for BitC in providing persuasive information is relevant, for the Per Cent Club is one of the agencies where the lack of ammunition is felt.

One area where the clubs might make a particularly useful contribution is on the relation between companies' headquarters and local community investment policies. Our interviews have shown that strong and well-planned leadership from company headquarters can be a very effective stimulus to local action – provided that it gets through to local level, and it does not always do so. We think of a senior manager, in charge of community relations in a large subsidiary of a multi-national company in good standing in the Per Cent Club, who was simply lost when asked about the implications of his company's national policies for action at his own level. Or headquarters leadership may in a sense be too strong. A number of our informants have commented that systematic plans and standard procedures developed from national level can be an inflexible barrier to new local departures: it may, they suggest, be easier to break in to the informal procedures of smaller and local firms. Discussion in the Per Cent Clubs of the relation between policies and practice at headquarters and out in the field could provide very useful clarification.

Informality has been an attractive feature of the Per Cent Clubs in their initial stage, and there is little sign that members wish to change it: but for the longer run, if their potential is to be fully realised, informality may not be enough. We have met suggestions that at the national level the Per Cent Club has lost some of its initial impetus, though members are not actually dropping out: that it lacks the resources to think strategically – at present, as was said, strategy depends on two and a half people with very heavy work loads outside the Club, able to meet and 'throw ideas at each other' only every two or three months – and that the Per Cent Club idea is not professionally enough propagated to be interesting and exciting to the media.

Secondment and volunteering from the workplace: ARC, the Volunteer Centre, and BIC
Secondment: ARC
Promotion of secondment, full- or part-time, has been the special field of the Action Resource Centre. ARC was founded in 1973 by 'a group of business people concerned about the divisions in society....as a means of bringing business skills to bear on community problems'. The lead came from IBM. Initially ARC specialised in promoting secondments, but recession in the late 1950s made this more difficult, and ARC diversified into other fields of community support, including setting up in 1978 one of the first enterprise agencies. In the early 1980s it lost some of its impetus. The arrival of BitC made it harder to assert ARC's identity, and for a time it had 'a very low profile indeed'. In 1985 ARC decided to focus again on its core activity of advising on and brokering secondments and developing guidelines for their management. It still maintains other services, notably in promoting Business Links schemes to bring together community groups which need furniture, equipment, and other community resources with businesses willing to provide them, but in 1988/9 90 per cent of the value of 'resources in kind generated by ARC' came from secondments. ARC focusses primarily on inner cities, and operates through ten local offices and a small national office, with a budget in 1988/9 of £960,000: mainly from local authority and government grants, but 25 per cent from company and charitable donations.

ARC obtains national publicity in a variety of ways: the informal business-community grapevine, mailshots, conferences, the trade press, BitC publications. Its approach to individual companies is direct and customised: it approaches the Personnel Director and makes a presentation on the benefits of secondment; then it listens carefully to what the company is already doing and prepares a tailored package of ideas on secondment opportunities. Success in approaches at local level was said to depend crucially on local networks and 'really good business connections', for example through Chambers of Commerce. In the late 1970s and early 1980s these networks were neglected, but big efforts are now being made to create local publicity through events and to build up the effectiveness of ARC's local offices and coordinate their activities with national strategic plans.

55 companies placed secondees through ARC in 1988/9, and the total number of placements was 174. ARC is far, therefore, from being the only channel for secondments. An ARC survey of leading companies and government departments in the same year found that 128 respondents were between them providing 1,040 secondments, but with a very uneven distribution: a quarter of the costs of secondment fell on the government departments, and four-fifths of the rest on ten companies. Companies which already have a strong positive approach to secondment may support ARC's activities, but have less need than others of ARC's services and tend to prefer to 'run their own show'.

ARC has hitherto concentrated on promotion among larger companies, but sees a systematic approach to medium and smaller companies as a key task for its next phase of development. This will obviously be a large and time-consuming operation - yet, it was suggested, perhaps in some ways easier than in the case of large companies, since, as ARC like others comments, these are more likely to have established policies and practices which can be hard to break through. Recently, ARC has moved towards promoting short-term and part-time secondments ('development assignments'), partly to make it easier to obtain the release of staff in mid-career, but also to encourage release by companies and partnerships with only small numbers of staff at the relevant level.

ARC's comments on the process of educating managements to appreciate the value of secondments, to secondees and seconding organisations as well as to recipients, echo those of informants in other fields. Too few of the organisations with which ARC deals have clearly defined policies and procedures. Too many still see secondment as a secondary and charitable rather than a mainstream business activity, react to requests rather than take a proactive role, and tend to use secondment as a convenient way of easing out people near retirement rather than as a useful stage in career development. The process of educating companies was said to be 'very very slow', with no quick-fix solutions, depending on hard work in developing personal contacts and using networks: and not helped by imprecise demarcations between the roles of promotional agencies.

Volunteering from the workplace: the Volunteer Centre, ARC, and BitC
A feature of recent American experience (Paper VI) has been the rapid growth of organised company support for volunteering from the workplace. This, till very recently, has been less systematically developed in Britain, though there are examples in a few individual companies, most notably Allied Dunbar. The Volunteer Centre has 'tried to light the American spark here', and in 1984 combined with Volunteer, its opposite number in the United States, to organise a joint course at Ashridge Management College on employee community involvement. There was only limited business interest, however, and little repercussion. The Centre's promotional journal, EC Eye, had to be discontinued in 1989 through lack of financial support.

Two reasons are suggested for the slowness of takeoff in Britain. First, the Volunteer Centre has had little direct business support, and when acting on its own is from the point of view of business an 'outsider', suspected of grinding its own axe, and not speaking to business with the authority of senior business managers themselves. Secondly, British managers and employees have been more reluctant than Americans to accept the idea that an employer might be concerned with what employees do outside their place of work: as survey evidence has tended to suggest, 'none of your business'.

But changes are coming. Our interviews confirm informants' comment that employees are increasingly ready to accept a degree of company involvement, provided that the company is cautious about crossing the barrier between encouraging volunteering and putting on pressure. The American example begins to be noted. A recent visit by Whitbread's Director of Community Affairs to the USA led to an innovative company policy which is likely also to be promoted externally. EC Eye is being replaced in 1990 with a new journal, in collaboration with ARC, to promote both ECI and secondments.

BitC, as noted above, has now started a systematic drive 'to persuade 100 of the UK's largest employers to undertake to create a climate in their companies which fosters ECI'. Pilots for marketing this initiative were set up at the beginning of 1990, supported with research on 'the benefits, perceptions, and vocabulary of ECI amongst employer groups', and the drive was publicly launched in June 1990 with an address by the Prince of Wales. Though it is aimed in the first place at large employers ('leading companies', as the launch publicity said), the target team responsible for it is working with the Marketing Business Action team which promotes community involvement to medium and small businesses. One suggestion is for a regional information network on the activities and needs of voluntary organisations, including the Volunteer Centre's network of 300 local Volunteer Bureaux, for the benefit particularly of smaller companies which do not have the time or resources to research the best ways of becoming involved.

A good beginning has thus been made, but there are still teething problems. Surprisingly, for example, the Volunteer Centre is not represented on BitC's target team. When a Home Office minister followed up the launch of the new drive with a strong recomendation to companies to allow time off for voluntary work, he attracted from a member of the Speaker's Committee on Active Citizenship the acid comment that the response of senior officials to an enquiry whether this would apply to the civil service had been 'get lost' (*Daily Telegraph*, May 5, 1990).

A focus for specialised Initiatives for employment, enterprise, and the environment: the Bridge Group

The problem of presenting a clear image and avoiding overlap and confusion is not confined to ARC and BitC. ARC is one of a number of specialist agencies which have found that they need to coordinate their efforts, and have come together with BitC in a Bridge Group to do so.

Project Fullemploy was started in 1973 on the initiative of two senior members of a City firm to bring private sector management and talent to bear, in cooperation with national and local government, community and other voluntary organisations, on 'the effective involvement of minority ethnic communities in the economic life of the UK'. Substantial finance was raised through City contacts, but an early lesson was that money, for the type of firms approached, was a minor consideration. What companies needed was solid reasons why this enterprise was not merely a charity but in the company's interests, either direct – 'peaceful streets are good to trade in' – or at least in terms of public relations. This point about 'reasons' is taken up again below in a more general context.

Instant Muscle (1981) helps unemployed and especially disadvantaged young people to set up their own businesses through a team of volunteer, seconded, and salaried business advisers in seven regions. The Prince's Youth Business Trust (1986) has similar objectives. Young Enterprise (1962) aims to educate young people of secondary school age in business organisation, methods, and practice through setting up and operating

47

scale-model enterprises of their own. The Apex Trust (1965) works to improve the employment prospects of young people who are ex-offenders or at risk of offending.

In a very different field, the Groundwork Foundation has since 1983 been promoting environmental improvement in and around urban areas through a network, by the end of 1989, of 16 local Groundwork Trusts in partnership between the private sector, government, and local communities, and involving large numbers of volunteers. Business support has become substantial – nearly £500,000 in cash and kind, including the value of secondments, in 1989 – and also widespread: good support from leading companies, but also from many medium and small businesses. In 1989 Groundwork claimed to have active support from over 9,000 companies in the private sector. 'Companies obviously see partnership with us as a cost-effective way of contributing to environmental improvement'. By 1989 Groundwork could claim that it had completed over 2,200 environmental projects.

At the end of 1988 these agencies combined with ARC, BitC, Livewire UK, and the Industrial Society to set up the Bridge Group 'to promote collaboration and joint action among its member agencies, and to increase company and government awareness of the many opportunities for successful partnerships with local communities'. The same comment can be made as on the new initiatives on volunteering from the workplace: there have been teething troubles, but a beginning has been made.

Promoting sponsorship: ABSA and Action Match
ABSA

The Association for Business Sponsorship of the Arts (ABSA) was founded in 1976. It is 'an independent association representing business sponsors of the arts, and aims to promote and facilitate the practice of business sponsorship of the arts in the United Kingdom'. It has been called 'the trade association for sponsors of the arts'. It also administers since 1984 the government's Business Sponsorship Incentive Scheme (BSIS) for matching grants for new sponsors.

ABSA's accounts distinguish three budgets. Its general expenditure for promotions and awards in 1988/9 was £217,000, financed mainly from business subscriptions and special donations. Its budget for administering BSIS was £261,000, met by government grant. This does not include the amount of BSIS awards, £3 million in that year. ABSA also launched at the end of 1988 Business in the Arts (BIA) to promote part-time or, less often, full-time secondments from business to arts organisations, 'general small business advice' to arts organisations, and training courses for arts managers. The lead came from IBM, borrowing as so often from American practice. The initial budget of £60,000 was met primarily from donations by eight major firms, but with a start-up grant of £25,000 from the government. ABSA has a London office with 17 staff and offices in Scotland, Wales, and Northern Ireland. The administration of BIA is being decentralised on a 'affiliate model' to local consortia of arts organisations, business, and local authorities or development corporations, affiliated to BIA but locally managed and financed.

In 1976 the value of business sponsorship of the arts was around £600,000 a year. By 1987/8 it is estimated to have reached about £30 million. There is some imprecision about the figures, and it is not clear how they should be broken down between donations and sponsorship primarily for business reasons: but by any test the increase has been dramatic. So far as ABSA's part in this has been concerned, BSIS has been the flagship. Over £6 million of additional sponsorship was generated in its first four years, matched by nearly £3 million of government money. Government grant is available only for first-time sponsors during their first three years of sponsorship, and it is reasonable to expect that some companies will drop out as the period of grant ends. But ABSA sees a key to the future in the way in which BSIS creates an opening for arts organisations into business, since the sponsoring firm and the sponsored arts organisation have to work together to set up an application. The point of the 'affiliate model' in BIA, similarly, is not only that it relieves ABSA of administrative costs but that it helps to 'move business people into the arts': to break down barriers, change attitudes, and promote a realistic view of the arts. Examples were quoted of how arts organisations in their turn take local initiatives to involve local businesses. The neatly roundabout way in which ABSA has supported the Thamesdown Arts Foundation is set out in our Swindon case study (Paper IV).

The arts, as ABSA would say, have a glamour and attraction of their own, though today with increasing competition from environmental causes. ABSA does not neglect the theme of corporate citizenship: company chairmen 'like to stand up with their hand on their heart and look warm-hearted', and the idea of corporate citizenship may appeal particularly to local firms. But it emphasises and capitalises on companies' own interest in sponsorship or in staff development through secondment. The approach here is very different, an informant said, from when I worked for a national association which was 'a vestige of Victorian charity'. Companies, as *The Economist* wrote in December 1989, are increasingly treating arts sponsorship as a main form of marketing activity, and one to be explored imaginatively: the 'Mozart factor', the safe option, is fading.

In 1989 244 companies and business associations were patrons or members of ABSA. These were mainly large, and, even so, a minority among large companies: only a fifth of the Times 1000 companies sponsored the arts. The total number of companies involved, however, through ABSA or BSIS awards or BIA or other local activities, is far greater, and many of them are medium or small, since BSIS awards may be as small as £1,000. ABSA-Scotsman awards in 1988, for example, went among others to Balbir's Indian Brasserie and to Norman Rollow Motors of Kirkcaldy: hardly among the industrial giants.

But ABSA's main problem in the end, as with other promotional organisations, is that businesses have to be 'talked through', and staff time, or time from volunteers in local networks, has to be found for this. You have to keep arguing, it was said, and get the right letter on the right desk at the right time. ABSA's staff is not large, and those employed on its regular budget have a first commitment to servicing ABSA's own member companies.

Action Match
The major charitable organisations have become increasingly professional in promoting sponsorship of their own projects, but there has till recently been a gap in collective national promotion of sponsorship of these kinds. Community Links was founded in 1977 as a general purpose community development organisation in East London, and developed over the years a national role in, among other things, promoting business sponsorship of social causes. This activity accounted for about one-third of its income, and in 1989 was hived off into a specialist association, Action Match, with an official ministerial launch. Its initial budget was financed by a group of companies, with a government grant to cover office costs during the first year. Future finance is expected to come from commercial sponsors, subscriptions, and service fees.

Action Match is building a data base and matching service for companies and charities looking for sponsorship opportunities, and supporting it with training, advice, and consultancy service in eleven regions, and through national and local publicity and direct approaches to business decision makers. One technique is 'regional business breakfasts'.

Time will be needed to assess Action Match's success: but it is building on Community Links' established experience, and in principle at least the gap in 'social' sponsorship has been filled.

Promoting business-education links

National promotion of business-education links is not altogether new, but changed into high gear as a result of the drive from the second half of the 1970s for a more enterprising economy. One of the obstacles identified was deficiencies in education and training: both in quantity, by comparison with competing countries like Germany, Japan, or the USA, and in terms of attitudes, for many government and business leaders saw a need for 'a positive change in the anti-industrial attitudes which can still be found in our society', and not least in schools and higher education.

School-business links

The Great Debate on education opened in 1976 by the then Prime Minister (James Callaghan) and Secretary of State for Education (Shirley Williams), was followed by a bewildering array of initiatives on school-business links. A NEDO report in 1985 mapped the 'schools-industry galaxy' in a diagram with 89 sets of initials, a number of them representing only the national tip of an iceberg of initiatives at regional and local level. Industry Year 1986 was, much more than usually happens with Years, an occasion for nation-wide promotions. Its momentum was carried forward by *Industry Matters*, a national campaign through a network of regional and local groups and a central team based at the Royal Society of Arts, and supported by all the relevant government departments, the Training Agency, and 29 other national promotional organisations. The Education Reform Act of 1988 added a statutory element, a new requirement to appoint or coopt school and college governors with business experience.

Industry Matters was intended to develop partnerships between industry and education, including links with all secondary and an increasing number of primary schools: action, not least by industry itself, to increase awareness in the educational world of industry's role and service to the community: work shadowing and work experience: and secondments from industry to schools and colleges and involvement of industrialists in teacher training. The initial focus was on colleges and secondary schools, but steady progress was made in reaching primary schools as well. During Industry Year around ten per cent of primary schools were involved with industry: by 1988 this proportion doubled, and nearly three out of five education authorities had policies covering the primary age range.

The Industry Matters campaign was planned to run for two years. In 1988/9 BIC's target team on education-business partnerships consulted some 250 organisations and individuals in business and education, and found general agreement on the need for a permanent national body to promote employer involvement in all phases of education, but primarily in the age range from 5 to 19. A Foundation for Education Business Partnerships was launched accordingly in 1989, with joint government and business funding and a council including leaders from business, education, and government, among others the permanent secretaries of the Departments of Education and Science and Employment and the chief executive of the Training Agency. It became operational in April 1990.

As our local case studies show, the campaign to develop school-business links has led to more widespread personal involvement of business people in their local community than any other form of national or local promotion, with a substantial commitment of time - over and above any other forms of giving in cash and kind – both within firms, for example in organising work experience, and in the schools. Incomes Data Services[1] has brought together statistics on the results achieved by 1989/90: 29 educational compacts involving 3,800 employers, a target of 700,000 placements for work experience, business governors in all the secondary schools where local authorities had the information available, teacher placements in manufacturing industry by 23 per cent of secondary schools and in services by 16 per cent, and the growing links just mentioned with primary schools.

A main reason for this good result has been the success of the campaign in stimulating local initiative. Local education authorities have been encouraged – with pump-priming grants, in some cases, as with TVEI – but not compelled, and have been left to work out their plans in their own way in cooperation with local business groups. Above all, the campaign has succeeded in in mobilising customer demand, direct from schools to local businesses. Schools have been expected to 'own' and develop their own business links, with local education authorities coming in as promoters and brokers rather than (except in the case of the new statutory requirements about school governors) enforcing prescriptive rules.

This experience is reflected in the terms of reference of the new Foundation. It is to *stimulate* the emergence of more business-education partnerships, *support* those which exist, *encourage* more businesses to become involved, and *articulate* the views of partnerships to government. It is also to develop 'a national framework which would identify national

---

1   IDS Study 456, April 1990. *Industrial Relations Review and Report* published another useful 'Route Through the Maze' in its issues of March 20 and May 22, 1990. One important later change, announced in May 1990, was the decision of the Department of Trade and Industry to hand over its school-business initiatives to other departments or agencies.

priorities against which specific targets could be agreed at local level in response to local circumstances', and monitor progress in attaining these targets: but through consultation and guidance, not prescription. In its preliminary consultations the Foundation discovered that the main reservation about a new national body, felt specially strongly by the respondents with most practical experience, was that a body which was prescriptive and directive rather than enabling 'could cause enormous damage'. The report of the consultation concluded flatly that 'prescriptive guidance to local education-business partnerships should be avoided'.

Industry and higher education: CIHE

The Council for Industry and Higher Education was founded in 1986 as an association of major companies and heads of universities and polytechnics to work together, build mutual understanding, and represent members' joint thinking to government. Time was needed to work out what the project was about, but eventually it focussed on enabling business leaders to understand the issues underlying current debates on higher education and to see the reasons why and the ways in which business might contribute. For companies of this size, it was said, money is not a major consideration: what they need is a reasoned justification for the policies which they might adopt.

The Council published in 1987 a first report setting out the case for 'a different kind of higher education system'. It should still be publicly financed – the idea that government might be pulling out was said to be 'the last reason' likely to pull companies in – but greater in quantity and changed in quality: more open, flexible, and attractive, continuing through life, with some shift towards science and technology but a strong liberal arts base, and with industry as an active partner, though as a customer rather than a supplier or financier. This initial report was circulated to and generally endorsed by a wider circle of 100 large companies. 'Senior academics and businessmen', as a follow-up report said, 'found that common thinking about the objectives of higher education had been developing, which was looking for a common language to express it'. The follow-up report stressed particularly the need for companies themselves to have clear Board policies on their role in and contribution to higher education, and to start by being aware of what they are actually doing. One of its main features is a three-page check list against which companies can measure their own performance.

CIHE was as a matter of principle set up as a one-off project whose continuance is subject to review. Companies, it was said, prefer the 'task group mode' to a voluntary organisation which may be self-perpetuating, with the risk of an unfavourable reaction if company support is dropped. CIHE has a small budget for its secretariat, and can deal directly with only the biggest companies. It has 35 of these in membership. But its influence is wider - 6,000 copies of the initial report were circulated. In 1989/90 it sponsored through PSI a survey of the actual involvement in higher education of the top two hundred companies.

Efficient giving to charities: the Charities Aid Foundation
By far the oldest of the promotional organisations, specialised or general, is the Charities Aid Foundation. It began in 1924 as the Charities Department of the National Council of Social Service (now NCVO), was re-named in 1939 as the Benevolent Fund of the NCSS and in 1959 as its Charities Aid Fund, and became independent under its present name in 1974. It now operates out of four offices, with a budget in 1988-9 (exclusive of funds passed through on behalf of donors or derived from CAF's own charitable funds) of £2,650,000, mainly from invested donations and bequests.

Federated and tax-efficient giving
CAF's guiding light throughout has been the concept of 'efficient giving' to charity, in the sense of relieving both donors and recipients of administrative problems, including that of ensuring that giving is tax-efficient. It takes in donations from corporations and individuals, claims the relevant tax concessions from the Inland Revenue, and either makes grossed up payments to charities as donors may direct or supplies vouchers which they can use to make grossed-up payments themselves. This service dealt originally with covenants, but now also deals with single tax-recoverable gifts under the Finance Act 1986 and Gift Aid (below).

Company donations passing through CAF rose from £3.5 million in 1976/7 to £7.5 million in 1980/1, £16 million in 1986/7, and £26 million in 1988/9. The increase from 1986/7 has been entirely in single gifts, which by 1988/9 made up half the company total. By 1990 CAF had 1,200 company accounts. Recruitment of companies to the service tends to be largely by word of mouth – 'one director speaks to another director' – but supplemented with contacts by CAF's own field staff. There is some bias towards the larger companies, which are more likely to have specialised staff aware of CAF's possibilities, but there are also many smaller companies which, as it was said, 'may put in a few hundred pounds a year'.

Employee giving: CAF and Give As You Earn

When the Finance Act 1986 introduced tax-deductible payroll giving, usually known by the title of CAF's own scheme, Give As You Earn (GAYE), CAF led the way in promoting the new scheme. By April 1989 91,000 employees from 214 organisations were contributing through CAF – by the autumn of 1989 there were over 100,000 – and the annualised value of their donations was £6 million, over 90 per cent of the total for all GAYE agents. Nevertheless, of the 150 major companies quoted in CAF's report for 1988/9 as 'Some Business Users of our Services', barely half as yet offered GAYE: and even so, as our interviews with some of these companies show, not necessarily throughout the company nor on a large scale. 'Effective promotion means face to face canvassing of individuals or small groups either by charity representatives or by committed employees', and CAF found that a substantial investment of time and money was needed to get GAYE off the ground. Its 1988/9 report noted that with a 5 per cent administrative charge – our interviews found some grumbles even about this – 'we do not expect to break even until about 1994', in spite of an unexpectedly high level of giving by those who do join the scheme. We return to problems over the development of GAYE below.

Community trusts: endowment, federated giving, or both?

Since 1984 CAF has promoted the formation of local Community Trusts. There were earlier initiatives of this kind, as in Thamesdown (Paper III), but a main impetus came from a visit by CAF's director to American community foundations in 1983/4. In 1986 CAF established a Community Trust Development Unit, replaced in 1989 with a Central Resources Unit. There has been strong American support in money and advice, and the Home Office agreed to offer pump-priming funds for the first three years of six new CT's. It has also made a grant for three years towards the cost of the Central Resources Unit. The unit's budget for its first 16 months was $250,000 from an American foundation grant and £42,500 from the Home Office, CAF, and the Gulbenkian Foundation. By 1989 there were 33 established community trusts, with another 27 under development and interest expressed in a further 35 areas.

In general terms, 'the community trust exists to provide a vehicle whereby all sectors (statutory, corporate, voluntary, and the public in general) can contribute specifically to their area': as one informant said, 'a bridge to cross', not least for corporate donors. How community trusts actually go about their work varies. The Hillingdon Partnership Trust raised nearly half a million pounds in cash and kind over ten years, and passed it all through directly to charities, as a matter of policy refusing to accumulate an endowment: a straightforward case of 'federated giving'. Thamesdown CT also concentrated at first on 'federated giving', with limited success, but is now combining with the Wiltshire Community Trust to seek an endowment for a Wiltshire Community Foundation. The South Yorkshire Trust has tried both approaches at different times.

American practice (Paper VI) is that the local organisation of federated giving is the business of other agencies, especially the United Way, and that the business of community foundations is to build an income-yielding endowment and use the income to meet charities' needs which may not be fully covered out of year to year fund-raising: and to build it fast, with money up front, so as to reach over five to seven years a capital of the order of $5 million, at which point the foundation is established and can take off into autonomous growth.

CAF has heard the message. In British conditions, it does not exclude federated giving as a role for community trusts, especially after an endowment has been built and a trust is well established, but the concept of starting with an endowment has gained ground. Experience has shown that attempting to operate on current income alone can be a chancy process, and some approaches to developing it have proved disappointing. Several community trusts experimented with GAYE for their own funds, but found that this gave too little return for the time and effort spent. Conversely, in the conditions of the economy since the middle of the 1980s there is a great deal of new wealth to be tapped for capital donations: and under Gift Aid single donations up to £5 million are tax-recoverable. In 1989 CAF obtained a grant of £1 million from the American Mott Foundation on condition that CAF can raise the same amount in matching funds by the end of 1990. CAF's plan is to divide the total of £2 million into three equal slices and offer them to community trusts as 'challenge grants' on condition that they in turn raise matching capital in the ratio of 2:1, giving them an endowment of £2 million each. The competition for this money is currently open.

The reasons why CAF has chosen to focus first of all on promoting endowed foundations are convincing, so long as it is not forgotten that there is also a case for promoting local 'federated giving': perhaps through community trusts, but perhaps on new lines based on American experience. We have a collection of comments by companies contrasting the 'fun', collective involvement, and morale-raising results of employee fund-raising events directed to specific targets with the unexciting process of individual giving through GAYE. United Way's model builds a whole battery of approaches to fund-raising, including payroll giving, into a collective effort within and between companies, and between companies and the community, which is 'fun' and does mobilise enthusiasm. It also provides for expert assessment of charities' applications: a problem for many companies if they try to do it on their own, and this is already a main selling point for British community trusts. The United Way model has been surprisingly little followed in Britain, and we include United Way International's own account of it as an appendix to Paper VI.

CAF as a pressure group
CAF provides a range of advisory, training, and information services, and is also a pressure group, actively concerned since the start particularly with tax incentives. It is not only concerned with cash giving: but, as a CAF informant said, charities are interested in money, and this today, so far as business is concerned, is getting left behind. In 1985 CAF founded a Council for Charitable Support with the backing of major companies. The CCS adds weight to CAF's action as a pressure group; the tax concessions in the 1990 Budget, for example, reflect its representations. CCS has also issued *Guidelines* on company support for charities, but has been cautious about the general promotion of company involvement, on which it could overlap with BitC. Its 'issue group' on corporate leadership is focussing in 1990 on employee donations and involvement and on the development of community trusts. We note in our overall report the creation by CCS and CAF of the Windsor Group to promote 'budgeted' rather than marginal giving by individuals and households and the possible long-term repercussions of this, as in America, on the attitudes of corporate givers.

Information and integration
The array of promotional initiatives and agencies and the alphabet soup of their acronyms is frankly bewildering, not least to companies: and we have still to add the list of direct government initiatives. Who is providing the Ariadne's thread to find a way through the maze? There are three aspects to this: straightforward information to corporate donors and potential receivers; creating cadres of leaders with a common understanding of the problems of their communities and of the potential for corporate involvement in them; and shaping and expressing a common doctrine of what corporate involvement is and should be about.

Basic information for corporate donors and potential receivers: the Charities Aid Foundation and Directory of Social Change

The simplest issue is about providing a road map, clear information about which agencies are in the field and what is going on. All the agencies described here are engaged in different ways and degrees in disseminating information about corporate giving, but there are two major general sources.

The Charities Aid Foundation has published *Charity Statistics*, now *Charity Trends*, since 1977, with increasingly comprehensive data on company donations. The main data until recently were on declared cash donations by the larger contributors, but results from a first Annual Survey of Small Company Contributions were reported in the 1986/7 edition of *Charity Trends*, and from 1987 CAF also began to collect, with some difficulty and often with a note that a company's returns are incomplete, data on the total cost of community involvement to as many of the larger donors as could provide them. We show in our overall report the strong case for fuller and more accurate reporting by companies. Our informants were divided on whether and how soon to make this a statutory requirement under the Companies Acts. The most common view was that fuller reporting should first be piloted on a voluntary basis, on the lines being developed by CAF and the Per Cent Club, leading to an agreed code of practice, with the possibility of moving on to a new statutory requirement once it can be precisely enough defined.

Directory of Social Change, in a different style of information, publishes every two years since the middle of the 1980s a *Guide to Company Giving*, with brief general information and details of donations policy for 1,300 companies, and *Major Companies and their Charitable Giving* with fuller information about company structure, business activities, and charitable and community programmes for 350 top companies. It also publishes a *Corporate Donor's Handbook*: a slow seller, but direct contact with donors is also developed through advice and training sessions.

Neither of these national sources of information, however, reaches down to the local level. Though information about particular fields – school-business links, for example – may be brought into focus by agencies at local level, our impression is that few people in any area are likely to have a comprehensive picture of local business involvement and of the problems to which it might contribute. Local information services are by definition local, but the national information organisations could give a stronger lead towards promoting them. A good though limited illustration is the move by BitC's Voluntary Initiatives team to develop regional information on voluntary organisations.

Community leadership programmes: Common Purpose

Paper VI describes the rise in the United States over the last thirty years of community leadership programmes aimed precisely at the problem of integration. Their purpose is to develop in a city or a county cadres of leaders from all sectors of the community, public or private, who have trained together over a year, seen and appreciated each other's problems and the range of problems in their community, and learnt to know each other and to work together. As successive groups of leaders and potential leaders pass through the programme, a cadre of eventually several hundred graduates builds up and forms a powerful and effective network. As more and more communities pick up these programmes – approaching 500 have done so in America – graduates moving to another area are likely to find a similar network waiting for them and to be able to slot into it at once.

The American approach has been taken up in Britain by Common Purpose, founded in 1988 from the background partly of the American example but also of the personal experience of Common Purpose's chief executive in managing an innovative training programme in a number of British cities and observing how in some cities, but not in others, 'things happen' through partnership across the sectors.

Common Purpose programmes were piloted in Newcastle and Coventry, aiming at the people now around age 40 'who are the next generation to run the cities'. By 1990 programmes for Swindon, Birmingham, and Bristol were in early prospect and around twenty more were envisaged.[2] £500,000 was raised from companies and government departments for the first two and a half years, but once a start has been made in an area the programmes are intended to be locally financed: free office accomodation if possible, and beyond this around £35-40,000 a year for each centre, including the salary of the local programme director. The point was made strongly that tuition fees should come from organisations' management development budget, as a matter of mainstream business concern, and not from the budget for community relations. 'Business people might spend 95 per cent of their time on the business and 5 per cent on community relations: we want to get across that what we are talking about belongs to the 95 per cent'.

2   Angela Neustatter, 'Something in Common', *Guardian*, September 5, 1990.

Local programmes are as in America locally developed and tailor-made to local issues and possibilities. Some initial irritation was expressed in Newcastle, it was said, because Common Purpose presented no national blueprint. 'I feed initiatives and then withdraw'. Perhaps six months of 'wheeling and dealing', it was suggested, might be the time required to get a local group together and set a programme up.

Shaping and expressing a common doctrine

But what, in the end, is corporate giving about? The need which CIHE emphasised to us to provide companies with 'reasons' for giving must evidently refer to reasons relevant to the individual company, but not only so. Practical men, as Keynes said, are more often than they think the servants of some theorist long dead. In a powerful article in the final issue of *EC Eye*, Peter Whates of the Volunteer Centre turned this the other way round: what the practical people concerned with corporate giving on Britain today may need is a theorist yet to appear.

> In my view the failure of corporate community involvement to achieve some spectacular breakthrough into the mainstream of company thinking can be traced to three key deficiencies.
>
> First, as far as I am aware, there is no real coherent intellectually based management theory of the business based case for an active involvement strategy, and as a result little or no academically grounded literature that would underpin such a belief system...,
>
> Second, and partly as a result of the above, there is not even a unifying vocabulary that could help to popularise the ideas espoused by supporters of the 'active business' strategy...
>
> Third, although there is now a burgeoning literature... it still suffers... from being largely uncoordinated, inaccessible to the casual enquirer, and often not based on any analysis of market place demand.

Whates calls for an effort by 'some form of quasi-academic body along the lines of a policy institute or centre', at 'a point that historians will record marked a crossroads in the concept of business involvement in the community', to build on the basis of companies' practical experience 'a coherent body of theory that would legitimise the concept of... the active business as a deliberate corporate corollary of the active citizen', and to disseminate it.

In a sense there is nothing new here. The idea that 'doctrine' is needed to guide practical management and express its objectives goes back at least to Urwick's pioneering work before the Second World War. Recent work on successful corporate management has underlined the importance of doctrine and the advantage to a company of being 'values-driven'. Business ideology does as a matter of fact develop informally out of corporate practice, and one visible manifestation of it, so far as the culture of giving is concerned, is the policy statements of a number of major companies on corporate responsibility and community involvement.

Whates, however, is asking a question about systematising the theory behind statements like these and propagating it more generally, at the academic or quasi-academic level. We have followed up his question with enquiries round some of the major business schools, but with disappointing results. There are courses with some relevance for corporate giving, and staff thinking and research underlying them. But we have found no centre which is engaged in the sustained effort for which Whates calls to crystallise out of practical experience a theory of the company in the community which would bring it into the main stream of management education and thinking.

The government's contribution

Finally, the government has made a large contribution to promoting the culture of corporate giving.

In the first place, the new emphasis of government policy since the 1970s on private sector and voluntary initiatives has been a pervasive background to the national promotions so far described, though still in at least one respect problematic even for active supporters of the 'enterprise culture'. We have found repeatedly a suspicion among company informants that in recent years the government has tried to unload onto industry some of its own proper responsibilities, and resentment of this. The government itself denies this charge. As the Home Office Minister, John Patten, said in the House of Commons on 29 December 1989:

> The government do not regard the charitable world and voluntary services as an opportunity for providing a cheap alternative to public services. I said earlier that I felt that sometimes charities are good at spotting gaps, but there is a world of difference between that and their being used for gap-filling. *Hansard*, House of Commons, 20 December 1989, col.581.

The practical conclusion drawn by some of our informants is that if this is indeed the government's view, then the government needs to define more precisely the range of responsibilities it does accept and just where it draws the line.

Leaving that aside, however, there is no question about the strength of the government's recent support for action to promote to companies the culture of giving. The record of one promotional agency after another shows how statements and addresses by the Prime Minister and other ministers have publicised and encouraged their action, and the value that the agencies themselves attach to support of this kind, whether in the form of an address by the Prime Minister on a national occasion or through ministerial support at more modest levels. To a small firm, as was said in connection with arts awards, it means something to get to meet the Minister. The Royal family, particularly the Prince of Wales, have also made a much appreciated contribution.

Most of the agencies mentioned above have benefited from government pump-priming or continuing grants or matching funds, and the government's own direct action, through City Action Teams, Task Forces, and Urban Development Corporations has been designed to promote partnership with the private sector and has in fact done so: though perhaps, as the Public Accounts Committee has recently pointed out, with a certain lack of coherence between government programmmes.

Most recently and most comprehensively, there has been the establishment of Training and Enterprise Councils (TECs – in Scotland LECs, Local Enterprise Councils). Industrial training in Britain has a history of uneven provision as between firms and industries, fluctuating with the state of the economy, and eventually needing large-scale support from the Manpower Services Commission and its successor the Training Agency. In 1988 the government decided, without withdrawing its own cash support, to place the main responsibility for managing training directly on business, with large implications, as our own interviews have brought out, for voluntary service by managers as well as for company cash contributions.

There will eventually be about one hundred TECs, independent companies whose primary function is to administer, on contract, what have hitherto been the employment and enterprise programmes of the Department of Employment and its Training Agency, with budgets for each TEC in the range from £20 to £50 million. Two-thirds of each TEC's board must be private sector employers at chief executive level. That in itself involves a large commitment of senior management time. Over and above this, TECs have a free-floating role through their Local Initiative Funds, which they are expected to supplement from local employer contributions or other sources – local authorities, for example – with at the start matching

£ for £ government grants, up to £125,000 for each TEC. Matching grants will continue in later years, though not necessarily on the same scale.

Companies' contributions to their local or regional communities through TECs, whether in cash or in senior management time, will clearly be substantial, and we have met some fears that they may crowd out support for contributions of other kinds. It is too early to say that these fears are justified, but there is some *prima facie* reason for them. There are limits to the amounts that most companies are at present prepared to contribute to local and regional causes, and £125,000, as one informant commented, represents a large slice of what is actually likely to be available in a restricted locality. Companies, as CAF's experience shows, are tending now to give less in the form of regular funding through covenants and more in that of single gifts which may easily be switched to new causes as these come up. 'Saturation is in the air', one informant said. A company informant specially concerned with the charitable sector commented that the government 'is really pushing the boat out with TECs', and was worried about the consequences for other causes in which he was involved. In a smaller firm the time-consuming involvement of the managing director in setting up the local TEC was reflected in lack of enthusiasm for allowing managers in the next tier to commit time to community involvement.

Tax incentives

Tax concessions for donations by and through companies have been progressively extended, notably during the 1980s, and overall, though they differ in detail, are now comparable to those which international companies meet in the USA. Landmarks include:

Finance Act 1922: seven-year covenanting: not intended as a benefit for charities, but proved to be so. It was already possible to transfer income to a non-tax payer, who could recover tax paid by the donor. This was seen as a method of tax avoidance, and a requirement to covenant for more than six years was imposed to limit its abuse. The change in the law attracted attention, and the story goes that 'the legal adviser of a Merseyside philanthropist' took note of the potential of covenanting for charities, which had been exempt from tax on their income since 1979. Surtax (now higher rate tax) was recoverable by the donor, not the charity; but relief on surtax was withdrawn in 1946.

Finance Act 1965: tax on companies' covenanted donations previously recoverable against income tax, to remain recoverable against the new Corporation Tax, at the equivalent of the standard rate of income tax.

Finance Act 1972: exemption from Capital Gains Tax for assets transferred to charities.

Finance Act 1980: four-year covenanting: the period required for covenants was reduced from over six to over three years: relief for the donor from higher rate tax on charitable covenants was reintroduced.

Finance Act 1982: payments to approved local enterprise agencies to be tax-deductible: extended in 1990 to payments to TECs and LECs.

Finance Act 1983: salary costs of temporary secondments can be treated as a tax-deductible business expense.

Finance Act 1986: tax to be recoverable on single charitable gifts by companies (other than close companies) up to the equivalent of 3 per cent of gross dividends: major shareholders in close companies no longer to be liable to higher rate tax on covenanted donations.

Finance Act 1987: payroll giving (Give As You Earn) made tax-deductible, initially up to £120 a year: raised progressively by 1990 to £600.

Finance Act 1990: introduction of Gift Aid. Tax to be recoverable on single gifts by companies, including close companies, and individuals, provided that the gift is at least £600, and that the total of gifts in any one accounting period does not exceed £5 million.

The surprise in this study has been the limited importance which informants from companies, as distinct from those from charities and other receiving agencies, attach to tax incentives. For receivers of donations these concessions are very important, but our impression has been that for most corporate givers they rank rather low in judgements about what is in any case a marginal item in company budgets. Certainly there was little interest in further improvements of tax incentives, at least as they apply to giving by companies as such. Perhaps companies had not thought far enough ahead: but our impression was that the first point for action here was not to devise new tax incentives but to improve some companies' perception of the incentives which already exist including the new and very simple procedures (relevant to some of our confused respondents) for Gift Aid.

Apart from this, the issues which remain on the table appeared to be more about individual and payroll than about company giving. Single gifts by individuals below £600, unless through GAYE, are not tax-recoverable in Britain, whereas in America they are tax-deductible. The difference here is important. American tax-payers make annual returns – most UK tax-payers, under PAYE, do not – and can claim deductions for charitable gifts within prescribed limits: from the Internal Revenue's point of view, a relatively straightforward operation. Under British practice it is usually the charity which reclaims tax, and the process of checking large numbers of small single donations against the donor's tax status would be correspondingly laborious. CAF has argued that the 25 per cent standard rate of income tax should be divided into 15 per cent payable in any case and 10 per cent against which charitable donations can be offset.

CAF has also argued for an increase in the GAYE limit to £1,200, and for extension of it to self-employed people: Michael Norton of Directory for Social Change has proposed a further extension to 'shareholder aid'. This may well be right, but what is particularly clear is that that, with or without an increase in the limit, GAYE needs more effective promotion. A Payroll Giving Association of the major agencies operating GAYE was set up in 1989 as a channel for representations to the government and a means of dealing with nuts and bolts issues like the standardisation of paperwork, but also to administer a government grant of £50,000 for the initial promotion of GAYE. Its members' experience, however, confirms that quoted earlier from CAF. The difficulty and expense of launching a scheme of this kind was under-estimated, and the resources available either to the PGA or to individual agencies fall short of what is required. There may be more than one answer to this. One, obviously, is to provide more subsidy to employers and GAYE agencies for initial promotion. The most effective policy, however, could, as suggested earlier, be to attract more and quicker support by building payroll giving into a more collective and less 'boring' type of campaign like that of the United Way. We have met companies that have gone at least part of the way in that direction, and with some success.

Our general impression, therefore, is that devising new tax incentives for giving by or through companies will be essentially a case of gilding the lily. The first problem, as regards incentives either for corporate or for payroll giving, is to market more effectively the incentives that already exist.

Companies' power to contribute to the community

Finally, there is a general point about the law. The question of *ultra vires* in company donations was occasionally raised. It is not a major problem. The old legal ruling that 'there shall be no cakes or ale except such as are for the shareholders' benefit' can be and has been stretched a long way. George Goyder,[3] however, has argued for many years the case for laying *ultra vires* to rest as regards community contributions by including in the Companies Acts a General Purpose Clause, modelled on American court decisions (Paper VI) and the policy statements of companies like Shell and BP, to the effect that companies have a general power to act towards the community 'in as responsible a manner as would be expected from a responsible citizen in the like circumstances'.

Conclusions

The picture that emerges from this paper's description of the national promotion of corporate giving is in many ways positive. There were doubts till very recently whether promotion of the 'culture of giving' among British companies could or would take off in a big way, but it has done so. The main fields of promotion are now covered or at least beginning to be covered: where there were gaps, they are being filled, and substantial and increasing resources in time and money have been committed. Agencies have in general a good understanding of how promotional action must work. Winning companies' support comes down in the end, as one promotional organisation after another insists, to direct personal contact and persuasion in the light of companies' individual possibilities and interests: but doors can be and are being opened by any and all of a variety of other methods, from general propaganda by national figures, or national campaigns like that on school-business links to mailshots and media advertising and honorary or cash awards like those operated by ABSA.

Further action on national promotion is still needed, and we have set out our conclusions about this in our overall report. We make here only three very general points.

Money for marketing

The first is about money for marketing. Though the resources already mobilised for national promotions are impressive, we have seen in one agency after another that progress could be faster if there were more staff for the time-consuming work of contact with firms or more money for other promotional action. Even the largest agencies are small by comparison with any substantial business, and the amount of extra money needed for staffing

3   G. Goyder, *The Just Enterprise*, Andre Deutsch, 1987.

and general promotion is modest, and within the range of foundations or companies as well as of government.

We expected at the start to find ourselves putting forward more expensive recommendations about tax incentives for giving, but have found in fact that there is surprisingly little interest among companies in improved incentives for giving by companies as such, as distinct from some aspects of individual giving. The problem here is more of changing perceptions and sharpening awareness of the incentives that already exist. We are clear that, if more money is available for national promotion, it will yield better value if applied to strengthening the marketing effort than if used to add to tax incentives.

The coherence of national promotional action

There is nothing wrong in having a variety of promotional organisations with different specialisations – so much the better, in fact, since the case for a division of labour is as valid here as anywhere else – but confusion is another matter, and we have noted the view of many informants that the distinction between the general promotional and signposting role of BitC and that of more specialised agencies still needs clarification.

Accurate information is also important, and we have noted here as elsewhere the case for fuller and more standardised reporting of companies' community involvement. But we put particular emphasis on another general need which is more easily overlooked: the need to develop the 'reasons' that motivate companies and companies' experience of successful projects into a powerful and persuasive theory of community involvement, built in to management education and management thinking. Theory is powerful, and we have been disappointed to find so little effort in that direction at the moment.

The national contribution to coherence at local level

All the agencies considered in this chapter are engaged in different ways in developing their own local contacts, networks, and organisation. The overall impression, however, is of an octopus reaching down with tentacles which may not meet at the tips, and this is underlined by the findings of our local case studies in Papers III-V. We have noted fears about imbalances which may result where initiatives are not coordinated on the ground: like the possible impact of local TECs on the balance of local giving or, more generally, the risk that as forms of business involvement multiply some, like support for local charitable and welfare organisations, may be left behind.

We are not saying that national agencies make no contribution to the coherence of local promotion: BitC's business leadership teams and CAF's promotion of community trusts certainly do, and so, evidently, does Common Purpose's promotion of community leadership programmes. But there are gaps. We have noted for example the case for extending business leadership teams to catalyse and focus business action in non-priority areas, or the contribution which national agencies like CAF or BitC could make to promoting comprehensive local data bases on business action and the potential for it. If, however, we were to select one form of national support for coherent local action which is particularly needed, it would be national promotion of local United Ways on American lines, as set out in the appendix to Paper VI.

III Business Involvement in a Boom Town: The Case of Swindon

Our three case study localities were chosen for their differences. Sheffield is a traditional industrial city with a strong local identity, but also in recent years with major problems of industrial change and unemployment. Hillingdon is at the other extreme: a slice of North London with a limited identity of its own, a 'non-place' as local people tend to say, but an area generally prosperous – though still with problems – and which stood up well to the recession of the 1980s. Swindon falls in between: effectively a new town, with a strong past identity which is being re-created in a new form, and with problems largely, though not only, arising from its rapid and continuing growth and prosperity. We begin in the middle with Swindon.

A boom town – but still with problems

Swindon is today one of the boom towns of the M4 corridor, with first class road and rail communications, a population in 1988 of 166,000, around three hundred companies employing over fifty, and an employed work force of 110,000 in its travel to work area. In 1989 it ranked 54th among the 280 travel to work areas in Britain in terms of current economic prosperity, and still more favourably – 38th – in terms of recent change and growth: Sheffield, by contrast, ranked 210th and 239th.[1]

Swindon began as a railway town, and its development towards a more broadly based economy has gone through several phases. In and after the

1 Tony Champion and Anne Green, *The Spread of Prosperity and the North-South Divide*, Booming Towns, 1990. On the recent development of Swindon/Thamesdown, see particularly K.Bassett, M.Boddy, M.Harloe, J.Lovering, 'Living in the Fast Lane: Economic and Social Change in Swindon', in P.Cooke (ed.), *Localities: the Changing Face of Urban Britain*, Hyman, 1989.

second World War manufacturing employment increased, especially in engineering, and in the 1950s Swindon was designated as one of the towns to take major overspill from London. In a second phase, in the 1970s, the tide of manufacturing employment flowed out again, and in the mid-1970s unemployment in Swindon was well above the national average. Service employment, however, even then grew rapidly. In a third phase, in the 1980s, the growth in service employment continued, and manufacturing employment again rose modestly even while it was still falling in the rest of the country. The last trace of Swindon's original identity as a railway town disappeared when British Rail's engineering works closed in 1986.

New firms have continued to move in. In 1982 there were 240 which had come since the late 1950s. Many of the newcomers have been American or other foreign-owned: by 1985 American firms were estimated to provide 6,500 jobs, including over a quarter of those in in manufacturing plants employing over 100.

By the early 1980s unemployment was again below the national average. It peaked in the worst year of the depression at nearly 12 per cent, but fell by 1989 to between 2 and 3 per cent. And meantime population growth has gone on: up by 85 per cent since 1951, including another 13,000 in the 1970s and 15,000 in the 1980s, plus a substantial overspill into the surrounding districts.

Growth and prosperity, however, have either left or brought with them a range of economic and social problems.

Some are about employment and economic development. There is less need than in the depression years for job creation, but in 1989 there were still pools of unemployment up to 6 or 8 per cent in some of the central wards, particularly among less skilled older workers. The people in the pool are not necessarily 'discouraged' workers: the Third Age First initiative described below attracted 200 enquiries in its first three months. But there is a degree of scepticism among them: they often need, it was said, to have their confidence raised. There is also, as the local enterprise agency, Great Western Enterprise, would argue a continuing need for help for small business development – though some companies, as will be seen, have their doubts. At the moment GWE is particularly targeting women.

In any case, high employment has brought a new set of problems over shortage of skilled and qualified workers, white-collar as well as manual. The number of young people entering the labour market is falling in Swindon as elsewhere. These changes have highlighted the need for new developments in education and training and in opportunities and facilities for women, notably the need for new provision for child care. The high cost of housing is a problem for employers moving their operations into the city or still needing to recruit from outside.

There are also social problems. There is more poverty than the city's obviously good earning opportunities might suggest. Swindon, as one informant said, is a two-tier city. There are those who are on the band-wagon, in relatively well paid employment in new industries, and those who are not. Poverty is relative, and 'in Swindon you know if you are poor'. The high cost of housing is a problem for low income families even more than for employers, and the borough is spending £300,000 in the current year on housing homeless families. What was called an 'enormous' problem of debt is coming to the surface through the Citizens' Advice Bureau and Thamesdown Welfare Rights.

There are social problems of another kind in the new communities of what is now a large and scattered city: the isolation of some mothers with young children (it does not help if the husband is a commuter), or of teenagers on outlying estates with a poor bus service and little to do locally; problems of single parents; and more problems than might be expected in a relatively new population over the isolation and care of old people. Parents, it was pointed out, do tend to follow their children into the city. One problem which has come to the front as the city has grown is the need for better transport and access for disabled people. The new Swindon, as even a quick walk through its centre shows, is not a place for disabled people to shop. And Swindon has of course the same general range of social problems and opportunities as are found in any town or district, from developing services like the arts to caring for old people and their carers or those physically or mentally disabled, or the hospitals' need for equipment and voluntary service.

There is thus no shortage of needs to be met in Swindon, and the voluntary sector has grown like the mustard seed to meet them. The number of voluntary groups and associations in the city is estimated to be around a thousand. There has also been strong leadership from the borough and county councils. With two brief intervals, the borough has been Labour controlled since 1945, but with leaders who have have believed in public-private partnership. Informants from other sectors gave them a favourable press. They showed vision and drive, it was said, particularly in the years when new growth was taking off, and have been likely to take a long-term view of development rather than to follow the 'flavour of the month'. The Conservatives have held the parliamentary seat since 1979, but this has not shaken support for Labour in local government. The fact

71

that the borough has been rate-capped, and now charge-capped, tended to be mentioned as an unfortunate limitation rather than a political crime.

What companies contribute now
There is already a considerable input into local social and economic problems from local companies and their employees. The main contribution of business and industry to Swindon is of course to provide its flourishing economic base, but companies and their employees also make a significant though uneven contribution over and above what the operation of their businesses strictly requires.

Donations to community causes
Though no one knows precisely what private sector business donates to charities and community projects in Swindon, an informed guess – it cannot be better than that – is that the regular total, excluding large one-off gifts and spending (for sponsorship, for example) which would usually be treated as a business expense, might be of the order of £400,000 a year. The distribution of giving between donors, however, is very uneven. Its curve is strongly J-shaped. One company (Allied Dunbar) and its staff charities contribute 65 per cent of the total. There are a few other substantial donors: either from local budgets or, if a company's headquarters is not local, with the possibility of larger donations from their national budget. Three of the other companies interviewed are members of the Per Cent Club, and a fourth could easily qualify if it brought all the costs of its community involvement together. But company donations then fall rapidly to perhaps £2,000-3,000 a year and on down towards zero.

Direct and federated giving
Most of this giving is direct. The Thamesdown Community Trust was set up in 1975 to develop 'federated' giving, through donations to the Trust which then uses its expertise to assess priorities for grants. It was financed originally by four companies, and 41 firms were members at the end of 1989. At least until then, however – a new drive was just starting, and a major change of objectives at the beginning of 1990 is recorded below – this CT did not attract as much support as a number of others founded since the middle of the 1980s. This was partly because it was under-resourced and run on volunteer help: it acquired a paid part-time director, with local authority finance, only in 1989. But it was also because the Trust failed to overcome an ambiguity that was apparent in company interviews.

Companies which are relatively significant donors could see the value of 'educated' giving through an agency with 'a reputation for critical appraisal of projects combined with professional advice'. A specialised agency like the CT might be better able than company staff to assess appeals from the less obvious local charities. One company, which has its doubts about federated giving at the local level, nevertheless passes a large part of its national charitable contributions through the Charities Aid Foundation, and called the appearance of CAF as an intermediary 'the great leap forward' in arrangements for company giving in recent years. But federated giving has still tended to be seen as a second best: companies prefer direct giving because it makes a clearer link between the company and the receiver. The Community Trust is suggesting to companies that they might split their local donations half and half between direct and federated giving, and at least one company is known to be considering this formula.

Informants also noted an awkward overlap at the time of our survey – since remedied, as shown below – between the areas of operation of the Thamesdown CT and the Wiltshire Community Trust, which has a full-time director and is seen as more 'ambitious' and more likely to think big. As one local manager said: I organised a major effort on behalf of the Wiltshire CT: then along comes the Thamesdown CT, and 'I can't cope with two'. That manager, however, was said by another informant to be one of the few who really appreciated the 'enormity' of the voluntary sector in Swindon and the problem for any individual company of coming to grips with it: which leads on to a wider problem about the voluntary sector. It is not only the CTs which overlap. For any one cause, the same manager said, there are five voluntary associations in Swindon. 'I tear my hair'. Why can they as well as the CTs not group themselves more effectively? Perhaps a comment based more on rhetorical hyperbole than on statistics, but he pointed to a real problem.

Federated giving and systematic promotion: Thamesdown Arts
In some other areas federated giving has made more progress, notably in giving for the arts. Companies may sponsor arts events directly, and the borough council has a track record in arts development going back to the mid-1970s. In 1988/9 the borough's Arts and Museums budget was £1.1mn, and a further £184,000 (excluding a special European Community grant) was raised for arts projects, 'organisations and companies'. There was still a gap, however, and in 1989 the borough and five companies (Allied Dunbar, Burmah Oil, Nationwide Anglia, Central Television, and Great

Western Radio) set up the Thamesdown Arts Foundation. The Foundation aims to attract company money primarily for an endowment from which to finance community, educational, and arts development projects, with a strong accent on 'hands-on experience for the community as a whole', as distinct from the 'more glamorous performances' which can attract direct sponsorship. The borough pays staffing, office, and marketing expenses. The Foundation's business plan sets a target of 65 subscribing companies and £350,000 accumulated capital to be achieved within three years. A systematic canvass of 150 companies employing locally over 100 was started as soon as a full-time officer was appointed, and at the end of 1989 the Foundation was on target for its first objective of 25 company subscribers by the time of a major public launch in April 1990. The hundred employee figure is not for the longer run a limit: smaller firms may also be doing very well, and 'there are a lot of rich entrepreneurs out there'.

The Foundation also links in to national campaigning on business and the arts. ABSA is developing its provincial network through 'affiliated offices' of which Thamesdown Arts is one. It cannot directly match corporate contributions to the Foundation, but is encouraging companies whose direct sponsorship does attract matching funds to redirect these into paying their Thamesdown Arts subscription.

Great Western Enterprise

Great Western Enterprise was formed in 1988 from two previous enterprise agencies, the Swindon Enterprise Trust and the Swindon Development Agency, set up with a British Rail grant at the time when the BR engineering works were closed. Businesses have given substantial support. GWE and its predecessors have never had enough free staff time or active support from their trustees to be able to reach smaller firms such as are targeted by Thamesdown Arts, but still can list 14 businesses as major sponsors and another 33, including professional partnerships, which have made smaller grants. Among other things, ten firms raised £110,000 to pay for a new one-stop centre for business advice and services in the former railway buildings.

But a qualification is emerging and the climate is changing. Companies could see the point of a drive against unemployment, but are more hesitant about backing GWE's current emphasis on promoting small enterprise. As one manager said: we haven't cancelled our subscription, but are now looking more closely at it, for why promote self-employment when we cannot get staff ourselves? 'Donor fatigue' may be setting in after companies have given support for four or five years, and a new form of competition is the need for companies to find matching funds to attract the government's grant for the local Training and Education Council. GWE has turned increasingly to generating its own funds through business development.

Business-education links
The most widespread form of involvement by businesses in Swindon is through business-education links. National emphasis on industry-education links dates largely from Industry Year in 1986, but Wiltshire County Council's INDEL unit has been systematically promoting business links with schools since 1975. Its working rule is that the ownership of link activities belongs to the school, and the school is expected to take the initiative and make its own contacts, using among other things its own local and parental networks: though with help from INDEL in marketing activities to the larger firms and 'brokering' links to reduce the multiplicity of applications to firms.

Support for schools and colleges may take the form of gifts of equipment or sponsorship of events, of very miscellaneous kinds. One company moved to a new building, and gave a school the plastic tunnel which kept its staff out of the rain between its two old ones. Another adopted a toucan as the logo for one of its products, and sponsored sponsorship by a local school of a toucan at a wildlife park. But the biggest contribution is in management time spent on teacher and student visits, teachers' attachments, work shadowing, and work experience, and on the governing bodies of schools and colleges. In 1989/90 2,100 students spent 20,000 days on work experience in the Swindon travel to work area in upwards of 600 workplaces in businesses of all types and sizes, down to the corner shop. There are no overall statistics of business-interest governors in schools, but the number is large: they are likely to be found through schools' own networks, and may come from any occupational level. In colleges of further education business-interest governors nearly all come from leading firms, including establishments such as the Natural Environment Research Council or Cranfield Royal College of Military Studies, and from top management level. Top managers may also be involved in other related activities. The general manager of one relatively small firm interviewed, for example, was currently chairman of the preparatory group for the local Training and Enterprise Council.

The time pressures which result for management in a period when staffs have been rationalised and there is little spare fat in the system were brought out in several interviews. Time commitments have to be rationed, and heavy commitment in education and training may crowd out commitments in other directions: as in one small firm where where the heavy commitment of two top managers meant that the suggestion that a manager at the next level might be nominated as a JP was looked at with a beady eye. Time pressures probably also account for another comment, that companies tend to be less proactive than schools in developing education links. The Swindon Partnership of leading companies (**see p.73-4**) played an important and positive part in developing work experience programmes, but it was pointed out that only a few companies have well-developed in-house programmes of their own, that it was exceptional when three companies combined to set up workshops for science teachers, and that that it is easier to find teachers for secondment to industry than secondees from industry to spend time in the schools. A similar point was made by GWE about finding young high-flying secondees to help in enterprise development, though it has been able to attract one or two.

INDEL is well geared into to the national network for promoting business-education links and makes its own contribution to national thinking and policy. It also attracts more active cooperation from organisations like BIM, the Institute of Directors, or the Swindon Chamber of Commerce and Industry than is found in the case of charitable giving and general community involvement. And the development of its network goes on. A major new initiative for a Wiltshire Education-Business partnership was being prepared for the spring of 1990.

Other employment and training initiatives
Business in the Community has been running since 1989 a marketing campaign, described in Paper II, to attract medium and medium-small companies into a wide range of employment, enterprise, and general community activities over and above those mentioned, and with considerable success. The campaign is proceeding region by region, and at the time of our survey had not reached the Swindon area. Meantime, however, some other local employment and training initiatives were mentioned, though they have been limited and spasmodic. Companies are changing their own recruitment policies to meet the new conditions of the Swindon labour market – one company, for instance, is offering women term-time work as well as targeting the over-50s – and this has led to some limited collective action. One company is negotiating with a secondary school for an after-school care scheme which will also serve other firms. Several companies and public service establishments are backing a scheme

promoted by the borough to set up a company to provide work-time nurseries: two are likely to be established in 1990. There was a Third Age programme under the Community Programme to promote employment of older workers. When Community Programme support was withdrawn, Allied Dunbar researched a new programme for helping older workers back into employment, and the borough joined in launching it as another independent company, Third Age First. The company has been mainly financed in its first stage by Allied Dunbar, but the aim eventually is to make it self-financing from employers' contributions. Another borough initiative for special training, the Pinehurst Training Initiative, has attracted some interest from companies, but marketing the idea to them has proved difficult.

Employee fund-raising: volunteering from the workplace
Finally, companies provide backing for fund-raising by employees and volunteering from the workplace: though, if one looks at the amount and form of support provided, the J-shaped curve of company contributions appears again.

Allied Dunbar is again in both respects the lead firm. It has a group of employee-run charitable trusts, with an annual budget running into hundreds of thousands of pounds: Swindon staff play a large part in these, and a significant part of their giving is to local causes. The company sees its employees' fund-raising efforts as bringing considerable benefit to the company itself, and not only or primarily in public relations. Employees involved in running the trusts were said to develop existing skills and gain new ones. Junior staff had new opportunities to show what they could do. Staff from different departments had opportunities not otherwise available to meet and work with others. A survey in 1989 showed employees' own satisfaction with their experience.

Allied Dunbar also has a highly organised programme to promote volunteering from the workplace, including released time and secondments, among others its ALPHA scheme for loaning professional skills to voluntary and community organisations. It circulates to its employees a *Volunteers at Work* bulletin on opportunities to volunteer, and in 1989 opened a new line of development by giving facilities for Age Concern to make its own presentation at company headquarters to recruit volunteers: with, from Age Concern's point of view, very useful results. Over the last two years, about three hundred Allied Dunbar staff volunteered under its programme.

Three of the other companies interviewed are forming employee charitable trusts on similar lines to Allied Dunbar ('We haven't been brainwashed by Allied Dunbar, but there is no point in reinventing the wheel'). Some are also moving towards, or at least considering, systematic policies for encouraging their employees to volunteer for community work, and three have at least 'put a toe into' ALPHA. Others may support volunteering for specific events. But systematic and well-developed policies for either volunteering or fund-raising are exceptional. Allied Dunbar's experiment in inviting in Age Concern for a presentation came as a surprise, though a welcome one, when put to a meeting of social service organisations. The Swindon Volunteer Bureau did briefly employ a part-time development officer to recruit from companies, but the experiment was badly timed: it was during the recession years when companies tended to be unresponsive (INDEL found the same with work experience). In the case of fund-raising the most usual situation is interest, goodwill, and ad hoc support for employee-organised events, through allowing use of facilities, carrying administrative costs, and perhaps making one-off matching grants: useful, but not at all comparable to the stronger and more highly organised programme in Allied Dunbar.

Companies' views of Give As You Earn are still ambivalent. One company has already operated a successful GAYE scheme focussed on a group of charities organised by the Wiltshire Community Trust. Another dropped GAYE but then relaunched it with some success. A third had done the same with little immediate success, but still with hope for the future: 'not our culture, but it will come'. In another large company, however, the comment was that there may have been pilot schemes elsewhere, but we don't know much about it. There was clearly a feeling about GAYE similar to that expressed about the Community Trust: the link between donor and recipient is too indirect and too individual – by contrast with the high morale generated in collective fund raising events – to be attractive either to companies or to employees. There were also one or two sharp comments on the administration charges made by some intermediaries. The company which had successfully relaunched its scheme had decided for the time being to absorb these charges on its own budget.

Could companies do more? Finding the right interface

There is no difficulty in identifying areas where companies might do more for the Swindon community. Age Concern, the hospitals, and many other agencies need more volunteers or secondees. Allied Dunbar's bulletin regularly lists opportunities. Shortage of volunteers was a main theme in the report of the Central Area team of the borough council's Community Development division for 1988/9. Community and social welfare associations of all kinds need more cash. Two joint work-time nurseries in a year and one school contract to provide after-school care sounds like slow progress. More could certainly be done in areas like targeted recruitment from the groups and areas still affected by unemployment, or specialised training, or housing for low-income and in-coming workers. Companies may buy houses for in-coming key workers – the borough dropped its own key worker housing scheme in 1989 – but one suggestion was that a combined effort by companies could provide a substantial amount of low income or employment-related housing which could be expected to remain so, since private sector housing is not covered by the right to buy rules which apply to council housing.

A list of needs, however, is one thing and a practical programme is another. Some limits are showing already, like the time pressures arising out of business-education links. How much more might companies actually and reasonably be asked to do? Four main impressions emerged in interviews.

Recognise the variety of companies' situations and interests
First, receivers as well as donors recognised the variety of companies' situations, and therefore that no standard pattern of community involvement can reasonably be set. The same commitment cannot be expected from small firms which are struggling to survive or from companies immersed in the details of starting a new operation in Swindon as from those already established and profitable. Companies' interests and motivations in any case vary. For one company a primary aim may be to establish a high customer profile; for another, to change unfavourable impressions resulting from its operations; for others, to establish a favourable impression of the company as an employer in a tight labour market. These are actual Swindon cases.

Moreover, companies' interests and motivations change. One reason may be the internal dynamism of companies' own contribution policy: our programmes, as one company said, lead on from each other, and the pattern changes accordingly. Companies, it was said several times, tend to prefer short-term commitments and specific projects to longer-term funding: 'easy money', it was was said of one capital development, because it was for a single project. 'They will pay for projects, not bodies'. Even where companies in practice provide continuing support for a cause, they may be reluctant to guarantee it, or to make grants for core funding for such, as was said, 'boring' purposes as administration. 'They like something to happen', and after initial support donor fatigue may set in.

There must be something in it for us
Secondly, while there is always a balance between ideas of social responsibility or 'putting something back into the community' and expectation of return to the company through public, customer, or employee relations, it was clear that, either up front or in the end, there has to be 'something in it for us'. At existing levels of charitable donation there were no signs of pressure on programmes from boards or shareholders, 'unless we were going down the tubes' – if indeed either bothered to be informed about these programmes or to give much time to them. In one company the staff dealing with community involvement were quietly conspiring at least to obtain a slot for their activities in board meetings. But even donations managers, let alone those concerned with sponsorship and other activities related to marketing, were clearly thinking in terms of company benefit. It might be incidental rather than primary: 'not primarily public relations', nor marketing, as one manager said of his substantial programme, but then he added an impressive list of benefits to the company which actually resulted. The point about benefit to the company might be negative as well as positive, as in the case of some firms' doubts about continuing support for GWE, or of the company which pulled out of a programme 'because the public could not see what we were doing', and, for once, some shareholders raised political objections. But the idea that 'social responsibility is good for business', as another manager said – enlightened self-interest – is always there, and perceived to be so by receivers as well as by companies.

One company illustrated the different approaches to which this can lead within a single firm from its international operations. In Swindon it plans its involvement to give it a high profile as an employer in the tight local labour market. Its Paris operation is small and lost in an area with little community, and there is little point in trying to raise its profile. Its German operation used to be in a large city, in a situation similar to that in Paris, but has recently moved to a small town where its status as an employer brings it back towards the position in Swindon.

Programmes can be effective without elaborate organisation: but many companies have something to learn about value for money from what they give

Thirdly, the question is not simply whether companies might contribute more. There is reason to think that many companies might get better value for money, for themselves and for the community, from what they already donate.

This is not to say that they all have to be as highly organised as Allied Dunbar, whose large charitable programme is managed by a community affairs department with eight staff, recruited as social welfare professionals through open competition. What is sometimes called 'emotional' giving in small amounts by small companies, on the decision of the chairman or senior manager with or without the advice of a contributions committee, can actually be well-directed and effective for that company's purposes. One large company makes a considerable and considered local and national impact through a large budget administered, very much part-time, by a manager and his secretary at headquarters and another manager and his secretary in Swindon, with the national and local pairs working closely together. This company recently abolished its community relations department as an unnecessary expense.

Nor does it necessarily matter if community contributions are spread over several departments and budgets, as they commonly are, so long as community affairs, marketing, public relations, and national and divisional staff not only make their own contribution efficiently but collaborate when that is required – except in one respect. Companies' attitudes to publicity for their activities in the community differ: some prefer to play it quietly. But in so far as they are willing to publicise them, and the activities of one company have a demonstration effect for others, it is unfortunate that so many have difficulty in presenting the total picture of what their total local or national contribution is. The way the picture is presented may also be unrevealing. We pointed out to one company that, though their national *Charity Trends* entry does give a figure (but incomplete) for total community contribution and not only for cash donations, it compares UK donations with world-wide profits, which makes the percentage of profits donated appear very low, whereas a comparison with profits in the British Isles would bring it well up to Per Cent Club level.

But there were also many comments from informants about inadequacies in handling the stream of appeals ('bandied about between departments'), developing programmes in a consistent way, targeting grants effectively and ensuring that they are of useful size, evaluating results to receivers and the company, and generally about the need for clear guidelines and adequate staffing for the contributions function. Contributions management, as one manager said, if not a full-time job should at least be a recognised one, not just 'taking people away from their ordinary duties'. Compared, for example, not only to Allied Dunbar but to the considered and strategic approach which British Telecom is developing in Swindon since privatisation and the re-grouping of a large staff into its main Swindon complex, many other companies have a great deal to learn.

Even in Allied Dunbar, if we may quote scripture to prove the devil, though the management of contributions policy is highly professional, the overall level of giving owes something to historic accident. The contributions budget is 1 per cent of pre-tax profits, plus a further 0.25 per cent to support employee charitable trusts. The 1 per cent level was established in 1973, when a director wrote a memorandum arguing that if the company gave, it should give significantly, and suggested that a significant amount at that time might be £50,000. This happened at that time to be 1 per cent of profits. So, 1 per cent it became, and 1 per cent it has remained.

But some companies could contribute more
Fourthly, however, when everything has been said about the diversity of companies' circumstances and motives, the need to find 'something in it for us', and the possibility for companies of getting better value from what they contribute to the community already, company informants had no difficulty in naming a list of substantial, established, and profitable firms which in their judgement could reasonably be expected to contribute more, in one form or another, if they were motivated to do so. There was no good reason why they should not join the circle of fairly substantial contributors and climb, so to speak, further up the J-curve of involvement. And this is to say nothing of the large but less well canvassed penumbra of smaller firms. One informant distinguished between companies employing under 50, which are likely to be struggling to survive, and so are poor prospects; those employing 50-100, which are time-consuming to reach; and the better prospects from those employing over 100. Yet INDEL does reach even small firms, and there are indeed, as was said in Thamesdown Arts, some rich smaller entrepreneurs 'out there': and even companies employing 100 and just above have been canvassed to only a limited extent. The interface between companies and the Swindon community could be pushed further

out, to the mutual advantage of both. How, therefore, is this being and might it be done?

Removing obstacles to company giving

'The door is not open - it has to be pushed.'

'Bloody difficult.'

'Bloody hard work.'

(Comments from receiving organisations)

The Swindon experience shows that there are no simple buttons to press to increase companies' motivation to contribute to the community. Essentially, as one informant after another stressed in different ways, the 'culture of giving' catches on from one company to another because someone talks to someone else one to one, respecting the other company's particular interests and starting from where some specific interest is. Inside or outside a firm, as one personnel manager said, 'it boils down to a marketing exercise'. It takes a great deal of time: informants illustrated with examples from discussions with particular companies. Beginnings may have to be small ('big oaks grow from small acorns'), taking hold of a particular point of interest and building from there. And, as the quotations above underline, there is no substitute for 'bloody hard work'.

The influence of a lead firm.
This means in Swindon especially the influence of Allied Dunbar: it is positive and pervasive, but can be two-edged. It can, as illustrated above, assist new initiatives and lead to imitation. But it can also scare off companies which are 'in our infancy compared to Allied Dunbar'. 'We're not Allied Dunbar' – or, from Allied Dunbar itself, 'for fifteen or seventeen years other companies have looked at our fund and gasped'. Allied Dunbar, though it supports both formal or informal local initiatives to spread the culture of giving, is cautious about being too 'pushy', or accepting that its leading position carries with it a special responsibility for action to spread the gospel.

Informal contacts and mafias are important.
There is a recognised 'Swindon mafia', a group of leading companies which among other things have been meeting for two years in a Swindon Partnership to discuss community affairs. The role of the Partnership as an

action organisation has hitherto been limited, and its main success so far as that is concerned has been in the area of work experience. But, as one informant put it, that is not necessarily the point. The value of the partnership is that it influences the culture of the area by bringing companies together: 'they need to mix more than just at a Chamber of Commerce lunch'; companies on the fringe ought to be brought in, and some at least are already 'getting the feel'. At the time of our survey the future role of the Partnership was being reviewed, with the prospect of a 'brainstorming session' and consideration of the possibility of more regular organisation and staffing.

The Partnership, however, is only one of a number of channels through which ideas are exchanged and possibilities discussed and the culture of giving is spread. Personal relationships count, an informant from a receiving organisation said: 'I have to take time to attend events, which is a bind, but that is where I bump into people and things happen'. There is a network of people in Swindon, in personnel management or community relations or in receiving organisations, who know one another and are in regular informal contact, and the exchange of ideas within and radiating out from this network ideas is one effective though not rapid way in which companies' involvement in the community grows.

Collective action may also result. One issue being discussed between a small group of companies at the time of this survey was on disabled transport. Another was the idea developed further below of a Common Purpose community leadership programme. Employee to employee contacts may extend the network. Two companies mentioned links between their respective staff charity group and social club, which, as a manager said, could be developed further for other purposes.

Extending and strengthening informal networks. A community leadership programme?

There are other networks in Swindon which have unrealised potential for informally or semi-formally spreading ideas about the 'culture of giving'. The British Institute of Management's local branch is involved in business-education links, but not in discussion of company giving or wider community involvement: nor ('In a word, no!') is the Swindon Chamber of Industry and Commerce. The role of the trade unions deserves further examination. It emerged in interviews as lacking in vision and leadership: supportive of the company's efforts to promote employee involvement, as one personnel manager said, but hardly in the lead.

There is also, however, a wider and more significant possibility, the proposal just mentioned for a Common Purpose community leadership programme for Swindon, interlocking with similar programmes in other parts of the country. The idea and American background of Common Purpose are described more fully elsewhere. Essentially its aim is to build over a number of years a cadre of business and community leaders in each centre who are familiar with each others' problems and those of their area (for example, to refer back, appreciating the 'enormity' of the voluntary sector), through one-year joint training courses. American experience shows that the network of graduates from such courses plays a valuable part in developing and directing companies' contribution to the community.

Two points about this are particularly relevant to a city like Swindon. One is about companies and managers moving in. Once the graduate network has been developed in a number of centres, in-coming managers are likely to arrive with a good understanding of how to appreciate and get inside their new community, and they will have a local network into which they can immediately slot. The other is about the boom town effect. Several informants noted how the impression of Swindon as a boom town can lead to overlooking many of the social and economic problems which remain: all-round awareness is what community leadership programmes are intended to create.

The possibility of a community leadership programme for Swindon is being studied ('within the mafia', as one informant said) by a group representing both the corporate and the community sector. This is a way of strengthening the local 'culture of giving' which could pay off significantly in the medium and longer term, and – though there may be some suspicion that it is a route by which business could take over the community – 'we see something in it'.

Systematic promotion of companies' contribution pays, where it exists.
One problem about informal networks and mafias, however strongly developed, is that everyone in them has other jobs: there is only limited time to commit. INDEL and Thamesdown Arts are examples of what can be achieved through systematic and well-planned marketing of company involvement through full time staff backed with adequate finance, and with a degree of national guidance and support. The staffing and money needed is not large. Thamesdown Arts has one development manager and a recently appointed assistant. INDEL began with a coordinator and a part-time secretary, and has since acquired two other full-time organisers and one part-time. The method of operation is different. INDEL stands out for the

way in which it has mobilised and 'brokered' polycentric school to business initiatives. Thamesdown Arts addresses itself directly to companies, locally or at headquarters as a company's own pattern of giving may require. Either way, it works. Business in the Community's national marketing drive, judging by its results in other areas, may well make another effective contribution to systematic promotion once it reaches Swindon.

A major gap in systematic promotion of charitable giving and general community involvement – but it is being filled.

Systematic promotion, however, does not always exist. There has been a major gap on the side of charitable giving and the involvement of companies in community projects: but it is now being filled.

The Thamesdown Community Trust has potentially four functions here.

- As a general promoter of company giving, approaching companies and talking through with them the ways in which they might be involved in the community.
- As an organiser of federated giving, particularly but not only from medium and small local firms and establishments: linking up with and promoting employee fund-raising and volunteering schemes and GAYE: very much on the lines of the American United Way.
- As a promoter, in collaboration with the Voluntary Services Council and Volunteer Bureau (the three are one complex, in the same building), of rationalisation of the 'enormity' of associations in the voluntary sector and of their approach to companies: as in the case quoted above of the combined approach of some local charities under one company's GAYE scheme or of the 'brokering' of schools' approach to firms by INDEL.
- And, especially if the Trust can acquire an endowed income, as the flywheel in the system of giving: looking after core funding and coming to the rescue in emergencies where 'donor fatigue' sets in and voluntary organisations are left in the lurch.

The Trust, as shown above, has not hitherto had the resources to do any of these things as well as it would wish, and there has been a confusing division of responsibilities between the Thamesdown and Wiltshire CTs. By the summer of 1990, however, the Thamesdown and Wiltshire CTs agreed to combine in a Wiltshire Community Foundation with effect from the spring of 1991. Thamesdown CT will remain legally independent for a further year, but in the final pattern there will be five district trusts, of which Thamesdown will be one, for the five district council areas in Wiltshire: each with its own trustees, to ensure local experience and assessment of needs, but controlled ultimately by the Foundation. The Foundation is entering the competition for CAF's challenge grants, with considerable hopes of individual donations. As an informant commented, a rather notable proportion of the wealthy citizens of England live in Wiltshire, though not in Swindon.

National influences also matter

The value of a strong lead from company headquarters and of good contacts and cooperation between headquarters and field staff stood out very clearly. British Telecom's new combined national and local approach (but this company is mentioned only by way of example) is a good case in point: national 'mission statements', including one on contributing to the communities where BTel does business, support from a group of central units specialised in community affairs, and a strong link between headquarters and field managers.

The value of national promotional campaigns was also clear. A comment on INDEL was that till three or four years ago the drive behind business-education links was mainly local, but today the balance might be set at fifty-fifty. As noted above, the influence is two-way: the national drive helps INDEL, but INDEL in turn contributes its own experience and ideas to the national drive. ABSA helps Thamesdown Arts, and Thamesdown Arts in turn is part of ABSA's provincial network. The Charities Aid Foundation, and the American advice and money behind it, touched off the proposed revolution in the status and resources of the Thamesdown Community Trust. Business in the Community promotes and supports enterprise agencies, among other things, and may well promote a number of other forms of involvement through its current marketing drive.

The government has played a direct part in some of these national promotions, as on business-education links or through its support for ABSA. One local criticism was about the type of support which it has given to community trusts. Home Office funding for CTs, it was suggested, has on American as well as British experience been too short-term to carry them through the period normally needed to reach autonomous take-off, and in any case has not been available for established but stagnating trusts like the Thamesdown CT.

On the whole, however, informants in Swindon were not addressing messages to the government about its specific promotional actions. But one wide policy issue did come up. The government, some informants said, should make it clear that it is not asking companies and their employees to fill gaps in what should properly be public services. Get the government's thinking clear on pushing more from the state to business, it was said in one company – how are companies expected to survive? Our policy is pragmatic, another company said: we do and should do what is right for us, and these things are not all the government's responsibility: but people do ask, 'are we being taxed twice?'.

Tax incentives did not figure highly in informants' comments. They really come in at the end, one manager said, when people already want to give: as in a church appeal where the vicar first softens the congregation up to give, and only then puts up the churchwarden to explain that if they convenant 'as a matter of fact the tax will come back'. Another manager from a receiving organisation said that 'in talking to firms I mention tax incentives last'. Nevertheless, some points about taxation and government funding were raised. Relief from taxation on workplace nurseries was high on the current agenda for some informants, but this has since been taken care of in the 1990 Budget. Other suggestions were:

- re-design of tax incentives to encourage companies to provide 'core' funding, though without precise suggestions about how this might be done;
- administrative improvements, like less paper-work on covenanting ('a pain in the butt') and 'more intelligible information' from the Revenue. There were also comments on the time taken by the Charity Commission and the Revenue to react to applications to establish employee charitable trusts;
- stronger and better-designed support for community trusts.

Conclusion

The conclusion of this review of company involvement in Swindon is straightforward. More companies could certainly be motivated to provide more support for local causes, in ways and degrees varying according to companies' circumstances and interests. But there is no magic wand for bringing this about. What is likely to be effective, as one informant at the centre of the local networks said, is not a 'monolithic' approach, but use of 'a number of vehicles' to 'ease companies into the corporate contributions scenario' and encourage them to make their contributions in the most efficient way.

All the 'vehicles' which have been mentioned are relevant: federated as well as direct giving; individual company leadership, networks of informal relations (perhaps with a more formal lead from the Swindon Partnership); development of a common culture among community leaders; systematic and properly resourced promotion at national and local level, on down to well 'brokered' and focussed initiatives by schools and voluntary associations. Swindon already has a useful set of 'vehicles' to drive.

We do not suggest that there should be any one driving force for these 'vehicles': a polycentric approach, as the informant just quoted said, is likely to continue to be best. But we do suggest that it could be helpful to have a fuller and clearer road map. It is easier to know where to go next if the picture of what is already being done, where the gaps are, and where new initiatives might best fit in is clear. We have tried in this survey to pull such a picture together: but we doubt whether many people in Swindon have a really comprehensive view now. It would be useful for shaping further action, whoever is eventually to undertake it, if some one agency, firm, or group, like the Swindon Partnership or the Community Trust, took the initiative to put the map of company involvement and potential involvement in the city together, publicise it, and keep it up to date.

But, however efficient the 'vehicles' may be and however clear the road map, no one suggested that the task of spreading the culture of giving among companies will be other than a long haul. Dramatic developments may occur, as they seem likely to do in the case of the community trusts. But, whichever channels of promotion are used, and whichever groups or agencies take the lead, informants agreed that what in the end matters is the hard and slow work of personal contacts and persuasion, addressed to individual firms in the light of their particular situations and interests.

IV Sheffield

Introduction

Sheffield was selected as our second case study locality for a number of reasons. First, it provides an example of a major city with a distinctive civic culture and economic identity. Second, it is a city which has experienced severe economic and social dislocation in the previous decade, prompting a wide range of initiatives for regeneration since the mid 1980s. Third, many of these initiatives have been based on a 'partnership' philosophy, linking the public and private sector in a particularly striking way. Fourth, private sector representatives have been heavily involved in supporting new forms of corporate activity in relation to the wider Sheffield community – for instance, in the establishment of the first local Per Cent Club in the country (see paper II for details of the national Club).

This paper begins with an overview of the fortunes of the city over the past decade. We then describe the principal initiatives, bodies and networks through which the private sector has become involved in community affairs and economic and social regeneration. Next we examine the achievements and examples of good practice which Sheffield has brought forth over the last five years, and also the outstanding problems in relation to company involvement in the community. Finally, some tentative recommendations are made on ways to build on existing successes and overcome the obstacles to more corporate giving.

Back from the brink: Sheffield in the 1980s

Sheffield still has its famous steel and cutlery industries, but its industrial base is changing rapidly after the hard times of the late 1970s and early 1980s. The traditional manufacturing sectors have become 'slimmed down', and services have grown in importance, with the headquarters of the Training Agency, the Midland Bank and the Health & Safety Executive all located in the city, and with major new service infrastructure being provided for leisure and retailing. More high technology industry is being sought, and many small companies are being established.

Much has changed in recent years. Our informants were united in their bleak view of the city's fortunes in the early 1980s. Sheffield was badly hit, first by the severe recessions of the post-oil-shock period, and second by the political in-fighting which led to a breakdown in relations between the Labour-controlled city council and the business sector. Unemployment rose steeply as the steel industry, the key part of the city's traditional industrial base, contracted dramatically. The city lost some 18,000 jobs between 1974 and 1986, and unemployment rose to almost 18 per cent by the mid 1980s.[1] The loss of several major factories in the Lower Don Valley, the heart of the steelmaking area, led to dereliction on a massive scale. The political outcome of the devastation of Sheffield's industries was bitter recrimination between left-wing Labour local politicians and the private sector, as the local authorities increased rates in order to fund public job creation and subsidised services such as cheap bus transport.

Since the mid 1980s there has been a notable economic recovery in Sheffield. The firms which survived the recession are judged to be more efficient and robust than before, and unemployment fell between September 1986 and September 1989 from nearly 17 per cent of the workforce to 10 per cent.[2] What has been even more striking, however, is the change in the relationship between the city council and the business sector. Since 1986, Sheffield has seen a remarkable surge of activity aimed at forging links between the private and public sectors and promoting joint action for economic and social renewal. How did this happen, and what initiatives have emerged?

The general view is that by around 1985 the antagonists in the city began to realise that there had to be a new consensus between the city council and the business community, and that new forms of dialogue and joint activity had to be created if the decline of the city was to be arrested. It was also clear that the image of Sheffield had suffered badly as far as potential inward investment was concerned, and that a new and more pragmatic approach to the city's renewal was needed. The extreme nature of the local crisis also brought forth what one informant called 'messianic zeal' among a number of business leaders, who began to work towards a consensus on regeneration with a new city council leadership.

Since 1986 a stream of new initiatives and partnership schemes have emerged from the improved climate of cooperation between council and business. The common factor is the strategic partnership between public and private sector in thinking about the city's future; increasingly, the partnership approach is being extended to the voluntary sector as well. The council and business groups have joined forces along with other players on the Sheffield scene to form an Economic Regeneration Committee, to set up a company, Sheffield Partnerships, which promotes the achievements and attractions of the city, and to draw up a strategic 'vision', the Sheffield 2000 plan. In 1988 an Urban Development Corporation was established in order to revive the largely derelict Lower Don Valley, and this has forged important links with other partnership initiatives. These and other bodies and networks are discussed in more detail below.

If the basic forces for change in Sheffield were the gravity of the city's economic situation and the change in the political atmosphere between city council and business, the process of partnership has been taken forward by other 'catalysts'. First, a group of business leaders who have acted as 'movers and shakers' in establishing links with the public sector and preaching to their peers the message that companies should get involved in the renewal of Sheffield. Second, a series of high profile projects which are designed to contribute to the city's economic base, generate new jobs and improve its national and international image. These include the construction of the huge Meadowhall shopping and leisure centre in the Lower Don Valley, the restoration of the Lyceum Theatre, the creation of a science park, the promotion of Sheffield as a 'recycling city' and, most spectacularly, the staging of the World Student Games in 1991.

It is clear that whatever economic fragilities remain in Sheffield, the city has come back from the brink over the past decade and has made a remarkable recovery, economically and in terms of its reputation and image. What is important for the present study about Sheffield is the way in which business has been brought into partnership with public and voluntary sector bodies for community projects, and the lessons this might have for other localities. Before looking at the successes and the problems associated with company involvement in the community, we describe the key partnership initiatives, networks and organisations which connect the private sector in Sheffield with public and voluntary bodies.

Networks and partnerships in Sheffield

The first thing that strikes the observer about the networks, initiatives and projects which link business, public and voluntary bodies in Sheffield is that there are a lot of them. The plethora of partnerships and new ventures is bewildering to the outsider and also to many insiders. However, the variety of activities does highlight the vitality of Sheffield and the sense of urgency which has marked the city's leaders over the past five years. The following is a brief guide to the main networks and organisations relevant to the subject of this study.

Private sector
The principal body representing the business community in Sheffield is the city's *Chamber of Commerce*, which has over 1500 members (around 10 per cent of Sheffield companies). At the strategic level, the Chamber promotes business involvement in the community through its role as one of the key partners in local regeneration initiatives. The Chamber was a founder member of the city council's Economic Regeneration Committee, has equal representation on the board of Sheffield Partnerships, and is well connected with other high level bodies such as the Development Corporation. It is a provider of adult and youth training and is a partner in the Sheffield Education Business Partnership, which promotes links such as the city Compact between schools and colleges and the private sector.

At the grass roots level, the Chamber sends a newsletter and magazine to its members, and these include details of requests received from voluntary bodies for donations, gifts in kind, and other forms of support. These are referred to as 'sponsorship opportunities' for members, and the Chamber publicises support given by members to voluntary bodies and individuals.

The most recent network to emerge in the private sector is the *Hallam Group*, a Business Leadership Team (BLT) set up in 1988 on an informal basis by Business in the Community and prominent local businessmen. The group includes representatives from the Development Corporation, Sheffield Partnerships, leading firms and the University. Its aims are to expand the number of companies involved in partnership projects in the city and maintain an unofficial watching brief on key initiatives involving the private sector in order to help ensure proper coordination. The range of the BLT's interests is wide: development of the city's 'strategic plan', the venture capital fund Hallamshire Investments, the World Student Games, the development of the local enterprise agency, SENTA, the development of the Sheffield Training and Enterprise Council, and so on.

Another BIC-related initiative is the Sheffield *Per Cent Club*, the country's first local club based on the example of the national initiative. It was inaugurated with a fundraising dinner which generated over £16,000 for the Prince's Youth Trust and recruited some 50 large and medium companies; the membership is growing gradually, and the target for the end of 1990 is 100. The club is a group of locally based firms which have committed themselves to contribute at least 0.5 per cent of locally generated pre tax profits to local community and charitable projects. The club, which is run on a part-time basis, was established on the initiative of the chairman of the Development Corporation and another leading local businessman. The club's aims are to demonstrate to the public that companies are involved in the community, to secure publicity for members, and to promote the culture of giving among Sheffield firms. The club makes no checks on its members, and in effect functions as a 'badge' of corporate commitment to involvement in the community. It does not handle donations, but simply circulates appeals around the members and leaves them to make their own arrangements with the voluntary groups in question. The club is not a fund in its own right either, but does aim to become a significant clearing house for the voluntary sector to use as the membership grows. Recruitment of members is carried out informally, via personal contact – 'the quiet recruitment of chum by chum', as one member put it.

This emphasis on *informal networking* is important in the Sheffield context. Our informants repeatedly stressed two aspects of the local scene. First, the role of informal grapevines in what is habitually referred to as 'Britain's biggest village'. Second, the importance of a network of prominent 'movers and shakers' from the business community, who have had a major role in the city's partnership initiatives since 1986. The names of Norman Adsetts, Richard Field, John Hambidge, Bev Stokes and Hugh Sykes are familiar to everyone concerned with business involvement in the Sheffield community. Between them, they are involved in all of the key partnership ventures and business groups and form a high profile cadre of business leaders.

Partnership initiatives in Sheffield

The partnership approach is embodied in the *Sheffield Economic Regeneration Committee (SERC)*, which is based in the city council. It is chaired by Helen Jackson, a Labour politician who is also deputy chair of Sheffield Partnerships. Formed in 1986, SERC includes representatives from the council, the private sector, the development corporation, trade unions, higher education and community groups. Its brief is to help coordinate the many partnership projects which are in progress and to pursue the city's unique 'vision' strategy, *Sheffield 2000*, which sets out goals for the development of the city's economy, physical infrastructure and cultural facilities. The 'Sheffield Vision' has been endorsed by all of the leading local private and public sector bodies and by central government departments.

Closly linked to SERC is the company *Sheffield Partnerships Limited*, formed to promote the city as a place to live and in which to invest. The company is chaired by Norman Adsetts, and there is equal representation on the board for the Chamber of Commerce, the city council, and the development corporation. The company has published a magazine, 'Success in Sheffield', to publicise 'the good things' about the city, including examples of business support for community initiatives and charitable activities.

The *Sheffield Development Corporation (SDC)* is responsible for the regeneration of the Lower Don Valley. It is chaired by Hugh Sykes, who is also involved with SERC, the Per Cent Club and the Hallam Group. The SDC, while not itself a partnership body, is nonetheless locked into the partnership networks not only by Mr Sykes' other positions but also by representation of city council and business leaders on its board.

As for partnerships covering education and training, there is the Sheffield Education Business Partnership mentioned above, which runs the local Compact scheme. Sheffield has a Training and Enterprise Council (TEC), chaired by Richard Field, who is closely linked with the strategic partnership initiatives; the TEC, due to be formally constituted early in 1991, is committed to working within the broad framework of the Sheffield 2000 'vision'. More generally, there is the role of the University and Polytechnic as a nexus for contacts between the business sector and the wider community. The University hosts meetings of a managing directors' club and a New Enterprise Club for start-up firms. Both centres of higher education are represented on SERC; the Sheffield Business School is a member of the local Per Cent Club. Finally, there are a number of companies and initiatives which, although not established by SERC, have a broad base of support and are imbued with the partnership ethos – for example, Sheffield Heat & Power and the Sheffield Information 2000 initiative.

Bringing the voluntary sector in

It is clear from the above outline of partnership ventures that a rich variety of bodies and networks has been created at the strategic level, bringing together the key business leaders and representatives of the city council, Development Corporation and other important Sheffield actors. However, the emphasis over the past four years has been placed firmly on making Sheffield more attractive for inward investment, on job creation, and on major infrastructural projects such as the World Student Games, which are conceived as 'catalysts for change', as one respondent put it, and designed to underpin industrial and commercial revival. Although the literature of the SERC and Sheffield Partnerships refers to community issues, several of our informants referred to a general feeling that the social dimension of the revitalisation of the city had not received enough attention in the new strategic fora.

After the launch of the Sheffield 2000 strategy, fears were expressed by a number of agencies that 'economic regeneration appeared to be of prime concern, with only lip service being paid to wider issues of health and social regeneration'.[3] In the wake of this, a Social Regeneratiom Group (SRG) was set up to complement the work of the SERC and to put community issues higher up the agenda of the strategic partnership bodies. The SRG is forming links with private and public sector actors as well as voluntary groups, and has held a conference on 'Quality of Life in Sheffield 2000', which underlined the message that social renewal needed to go hand in hand with economic revival.

Networking and partnership projects involving the voluntary sector have otherwise been confined to the operational level of activity rather than the policy making area, and are more modest than most of the initiatives overseen by the strategic groupings.

The most notable recent ventures have revolved around the World Student Games, which have always been seen as a major project designed to benefit the entire community and leave a permanent legacy of facilities. The company set up by the council to run the games, Universiade GB (now wound up and replaced by the city authorities and the Sports Council), aimed to get community groups involved in the project. The intention is to ensure that it leaves behind not just physical infrastructure but also community projects and a lasting 'culture of relationships' linking business and voluntary groups. A small team was set up to handle community relations, and extensive discussions took place with community groups. Networks were built up linking voluntary groups, city council departments and business sponsors in two main areas - disability and the environment. More programmes would have been established but for the severe financial problems which have plagued the Games' organisers.[4] Business support has taken the form of cash donations, secondments, volunteering, training and sponsorship of activities.

Links with the business community are also being made by the local Council for Voluntary Service, Voluntary Action Sheffield (VAS), and a community trust set up in 1987, the South Yorkshire Foundation (SYF). VAS acts as a development and coordination body for the voluntary sector. The SYF, as well as building up funds for immediate use and seeking an endowment, aims to act as a clearing house for charitable requests to businesses and a broker for company giving. The SYF and VAS are collaborating in the establishment of an information service on funding for the voluntary sector in the area, and SYF works closely with councils for voluntary service thoughout the region.

The SYF and VAS are also involved in two networks which draw in representatives of the private sector for discussion with voluntary groups at the operational level. One is the city council's Funding Forum, which provides a meeting point for community groups, funding departments from the council, and invited representatives from business (for instance, from the Chamber of Commerce and the Per Cent Club). The other is a very new forum, not yet firmly established, of funders of voluntary groups and intermediaries linking the private, public and voluntary sector. The first meeting, convened by VAS, brought together representatives of the Chamber of Commerce, the South Yorkshire Foundation, council departments, the Per Cent Club, and the Church Urban Fund. The aim of the network, which will meet quarterly, is to improve information exchange and coordination of activities at the operational level between the participants.

Sheffield as a model: achievements and good practice
There is no doubt that Sheffield merits serious attention from other localities seeking to improve links between the business sector and the wider community. The city's image has been radically improved over the last five years and a highly impressive range of partnership ventures has been developed. What are the key success stories relevant to the task of improving business involvement in the community, and what models of good practice does Sheffield have to offer?

The most striking development has been the emergence of the 'partnership' philosophy and the way in which this has been applied to major initiatives on economic renewal, infrastructural investment, environmental improvements, education and training, and the city's strategic vision document. While some informants pointed out that of course the political divisions of the past have not been entirely overcome, it is clear that the spirit of cooperation which has been achieved is genuine and admirable.

The partnership approach has been put into practice in the shape of a cluster of ambitious projects designed to make Sheffield an attractive and dynamic place in which to live and invest. For all its financial problems, the World Student Games has been a significant catalytic factor in bringing private sector resources into infrastructural renewal and community projects. Other initiatives, such as the renovation of the Lyceum Theatre, have also caught the imagination of members of the business community. The partnership approach to the city's housing problems has been innovative and successful.[5] The development of the city's own 'strategic plan', the Sheffield 2000 'vision', is a notable innovation and provides a broad framework into which all of the partnership projects can fit.

Sheffield has developed an extensive and effective cluster of networks linking the private sector and the public sector at a strategic level. The establishment of Sheffield Partnerships Limited and the Sheffield Economic Regeneration Committee, and the overlapping memberships of the boards of the various partnership bodies, can provide valuable lessons and examples of good practice at the strategic level to other localities. In Sheffield the key business and public sector organisations interlock in a fruitful way and valuable formal networks have grown up to complement the informal ones which link private and public sector leaders. This process has been helped considerably by the presence of a number of high-profile local businessmen who have been closely associated with all of the partnership ventures since the mid 1980s : their commitment has meant that the private sector has had a key role in thinking about economic and social regeneration in the city. Moreover, their ubiquity has provided continuity in the private sector contribution at the strategic level over recent years. A further source of strength has been the fact that the partnership initiatives have been home-grown – nothing has been imposed by individuals or bodies which lack a Sheffield connection. Moreover, care has been taken to try to integrate the Government-backed Development Corporation, which was imposed on the city, into the local high level networks.

At the operational level, several informants argued that large scale projects such as the World Student Games were likely to leave many companies with the 'taste' for further community involvement; successful experience with volunteering, secondments and sponsorship would provide fertile ground for a 'culture of relationships', as one respondent put it, to develop between firms and voluntary sector groups. We heard from a number of informants that voluntary groups were more willing than they had once been to approach the private sector and develop partnership projects. The voluntary scene has also been strengthened by the move towards better networking between funding bodies and intermediaries: in particular, by the plan to set up a funding information and advice service run by the South Yorkshire Foundation and Voluntary Action Sheffield; and by the establishment of a forum linking actors such as these with the

Chamber of Commerce, city council funding departments, and bodies such as the Church Urban Fund.

Finally, Sheffield has been the first city to establish a local Per Cent Club, and this should be a model for other localities to copy. Informants pointed out that the local dimension made the concept of the club much more appealing to companies : commitment to corporate giving via membership of the national Per Cent Club was, some argued, potentially too abstract and reminiscent of GAYE to be a powerful attraction to firms. The commitment to direct a percentage of locally generated profits to local community causes was much more likely to inspire enthusiasm among senior managers and employees. Moreover, the concept of the Per Cent Club is simple and can appeal to companies of all types: as one informant put it, the 'little guys' can also feel that they are playing their part. The local club is run with the minimum of bureaucracy and has the potential to develop into a clearing house for the voluntary sector to use in making its approaches to Sheffield companies. It also has a valuable part to play in providing a framework in which firms can work out how much they should be doing as one company chairman put it, 'you turn to that with some relief', since many senior managers 'really are lost' when trying to formulate a policy on charitable donations and community support.

Problems and some recommendations for further development

Despite the many achievements outlined above, there are a number of notable problems in Sheffield concerning business involvement in the community. These are discussed below and we make recommendations for measures to overcome them. To some extent the difficulties identified by our informants echo points made in the other case study localities and at national level; others have arisen from the particular pattern of development seen in Sheffield over recent years.

One issue raised by many respondents in companies and voluntary bodies was the potential for confusion and 'reinvention of the wheel' in the city given the proliferation of initiatives and the establishment of new networks such as the Business Leadership Team. Some respondents argued for tighter coordination of the partnership ventures and business-led projects, and for someone 'to tie it all together'. Against this, others argued strongly that attempts at rationalisation would be misplaced and could stifle valuable initiatives which depended on individuals' sense of 'ownership'; it was better to let people be 'kings in their own operation'.

To some extent the confusion prevalent among some respondents in firms and voluntary groups is inevitable, given that so many of the Sheffield initiatives on business involvement in the community have sprung up only in the last four years and at such a rapid rate. The sheer amount of activity in the city can also contribute to a sense of confusion and a suspicion that much duplication is going on. In general it is clear that coordination is good at the strategic level, with the key players involved in a number of bodies, and with the general vision statement of Sheffield 2000 acting as a further means of high level coordination: new bodies such as the TEC subscribe to its broad objectives. To establish yet another partnership group to oversee all of the others would be superfluous. It would seem better to recognise that Sheffield has enough strategic networks and partnership bodies, and to concentrate on improving the flows of information between them and to the actors most likely to find them confusing – namely businesses and voluntary groups.

There is a particular problem in this respect for the new Business Leadership Team, which has struggled to find a niche in the Sheffield scene. Several respondents referred to it as a 'mysterious body' whose role was unclear; others viewed with suspicion as yet another strategic forum – 'a Johnny-come-lately' – wholly superfluous to the city's requirements. Certainly it seems inappropriate for the BLT to aim to act as a general high level body for coordination of the many partnership initiatives. This may be a suitable task for BLTs in localities which have yet to embark on the partnership approach to community renewal, but Sheffield was already well equipped with mechanisms for coordination and discussion between private and public sector leaders when the BLT was set up. A more appropriate role for the Sheffield BLT, suggested by one informant, may be as a forum within the private sector for companies wishing to develop their community involvement, with a particular mission to recruit more companies to the cause of partnership projects and Per Cent Club membership. We consider that this is the right way for the BLT to develop in Sheffield, and stress the need for it to liaise as closely as possible with existing private sector fora, above all the Chamber of Commerce, which has begun to make connections with the voluntary and public sectors at the operational level.

The main gap at the strategic level in recent years has been the relative lack of attention paid to the pressing social issues (such as long-term unemployment and the problems of ethnic groups) and to the role of the voluntary sector. This problem was acknowledged by informants from all sectors; some argued that it was inevitable that the key economic and infrastructural problems should have received priority so far, since social renewal could not occur without a restored industrial and commercial base in the city. Others felt that the business community was unlikely to take an interest in the more complex and controversial problems confronting the voluntary sector, since these were not amenable to project-based solutions and did not have the same appeal to business self-interest as the big infrastructural initiatives underway in Sheffield.

The gap at the strategic level now appears to have been filled with the establishment of the Social Regeneration Group. Clearly one of the tasks for the Group will be to stimulate debate on how the business sector can be persuaded to play an appropriate role in supporting social regeneration initiatives. It remains to be seen how effective it can be in raising the profile of what one informant called 'messy' social issues on the agenda of the partnership bodies; but clearly its arrival is a welcome and potentially important development, which will bring the voluntary sector more effectively into the high level networks as a partner of business and public sector leaders.

If Sheffield is thus well catered for at the strategic level for partnerships and networks involving the private sector in community affairs, there is much room for improvement in information flows and opportunities for different groups to meet at the operational level. There are several issues here: the need for better coordination within the different sectors, the need for more communication between them, and the need for resources to facilitate this.

Many informants noted that the chief weakness in the private sector's role in community ventures in Sheffield was that relatively few business leaders were involved. The key 'movers and shakers' had achieved a great deal, but their resources were now being spread too thinly: they were invited to join every initiative, which meant that they were too 'stretched' to be truly effective in all they did. Moreover, their ubiquity could be used as an excuse by others not to get involved – either on the grounds that the high profile leaders were taking care of everything, or because of weariness with seeing the same faces – 'not him again'.

There is thus an urgent need to recruit more local business leaders to the cause of community involvement and expand the ranks of activists in the private sector. There is an important role here for the BLT, the Chamber of Commerce and the Per Cent Club to put more resources into marketing and recruitment. The Per Cent Club in particular is potentially an excellent vehicle for recruitment, but it has few resources for marketing and has yet to reach 100 members out of a business community of some 17,000 firms. Moreover, its members are largely organisations which were already part of the 'culture of giving'; the club has yet to bring in new donors on a large scale. Most firms in the locality, our respondents felt, clearly remain ad hoc and reactive in their approach to community involvement or are simply unaware and inactive. More could be done to reach small firms and to provide publicity for businesses involved in community support, but the hard work of networking and recruiting needs more time, people and money than are currently available to the private sector bodies. Putting more effort into recruitment would pay off, according to informants from industry and intermediary bodies: there was scope for getting many more firms involved, but they had to be approached on a personal basis and given coherent reasons why they should do more for the community.

Within the public and voluntary sectors several respondents identified a need for better information flows between individuals and organisations, and all underlined the problem of shortage of time for the 'hard slog' of making contacts and setting up meetings. This was particularly the case within the voluntary sector, which a number of informants felt was weakened by its lack of a strong and well-established umbrella group, by fragmentation among community groups, and by a general shortage of time and money for extensive networking. However, there are several positive developments: the existence of the city council's funding forum for voluntary bodies; the establishment of the SRG, which may help improve information exchange at the policy making level between the voluntary sector and its partners; and the cooperation between the South Yorkshire Foundation and Voluntary Action Sheffield on an information and advice service for local groups.

As for communication between the different sectors, the establishment of the quarterly forum of funding bodies, umbrella groups and intermediaries is highly welcome; it needs to be made secure and well-resourced, since, as several respondents noted, such initiatives are fragile because of the many competing demands on participants' time. Links between such bodies as the Per Cent Club and voluntary sector brokers such as SYF are to be encouraged in order to make them more effective in their roles as 'clearing houses' for requests from voluntary groups and offers from companies. VAS has already acted in this way with the Chamber of Commerce, which at one stage passed on requests for specific items and put a 'shopping list' in its bulletin to members. Links such as this deserve to be promoted, but need time and commitment if they are to flourish.

Given that bodies such as the Per Cent Club and the SYF are so new and relatively unknown in the area, attention also needs to be paid to improving communications between individual firms and voluntary groups. The key need here, according to many respondents, is for more resources to be made available to voluntary bodies to help them market themselves effectively to business; there is a great need for training on the appropriate ways to approach firms, conduct business with them and develop new forms of partnership.

How can improvements be made at the operational level, so that Sheffield's success in developing strategic partnerships and information networks can be replicated nearer to the grass roots? The main need in the city, as we have found elsewhere, is for more resources to be put into marketing, training and the labour- and time-intensive task of networking and recruiting senior managers and their employees into the circles of business leaders and into community involvement. Bodies such as the Per Cent Club and the South Yorkshire Foundation need more resources to market themselves and recruit more businesses to the cause, and to provide voluntary bodies with the information and skills they need to make effective approaches to business. Although the absence of national promotional bodies may not have hindered, and may well have helped, the development of Sheffield's strategic partnerships, they could play a helpful role in strengthening links at the operational level. Bodies such as ARC could be effective locally in providing specialist expertise, provided they integrated themselves well in the Sheffield networks. Business in the Community is not well regarded by many of our informants, who take the view that it has been ineffectual in its interventions in Sheffield to date; but BitC could yet have a role to play as a source of advice and resources for existing umbrella groups and initiatives in the city. One informant argued strongly for the introduction of a well-backed 'catalyst' who understood both private and voluntary sectors, who would work with the available bodies and networks in improving the flow of information and helping to market the idea of community involvement to businesses. Such a person could come from, or be financed by, Business in the Community, and would be based in one of the partnership groups – for instance, in the Social Regeneration Group, to allow access to the key local players at a policy-making level as well as at the grassroots. This idea found favour with respondents from all sectors, and we feel that it is worth further consideration.

Conclusion
Sheffield has the same problems associated with business involvement in the community as we have found elsewhere: low levels of awareness and activity among the mass of firms, a lack of skills and marketing resources in the voluntary sector for dealing with business, inadequate information flows between business and voluntary sectors, and so on. However, it has

achieved a great deal at the strategic level in fostering partnerships between private and public sectors, and these are now beginning to bring the voluntary sector in to a greater extent. The city's partnership initiatives and its local Per Cent Club deserve close attention elsewhere. A cadre of high-powered business leaders has emerged and played a key role in stimulating the ambitious economic and infrastructural projects now taking shape. There is much to be consolidated here: a new generation of business activists needs to be developed, many more firms have to be brought into networks such as the local Per Cent Club; social regeneration needs to be given a higher priority by the partnership fora; and stronger links should be built at the operational level between companies and the voluntary sector. No new bodies or initiatives are required for this; existing groups and networks just need more time and resources for the hard work of building up the culture of corporate involvement in the community.

References

1. *Financial Times*, special survey of Sheffield, 8 September 1989, p.1.
2. See 'From steel to shopping', *The Economist*, 30 June 1990, pp.35-36.
3. Voluntary Action Sheffield, *Voluntary Action News*, April/May 1990.
4. On the background to the Games, see *Financial Times*, op.cit., p.6.
5. For a case study on the partnership approach to housing in Sheffield, see M. Carley, *Housing and Neighbourhood Renewal*, London, Policy Studies Institute, 1990, pp.206-217.

V Hillingdon – Growing Together

'Hillingdon is not a place'.

'An administrative unit, not a town.'

'Hillingdon is nowhere'.

'None of us live here.'

[Comments from local managers]

The London Borough of Hillingdon was selected as one of our case study areas because, by contrast with Sheffield or Swindon, it does not have a clearly defined identity. It was put together in 1965 out of four districts which did have an identity, and this is still reflected in the district by district organisation of Chambers of Trade and Commerce, of some voluntary social services, and in the arts.

Hillingdon has a fairly well marked western boundary, but on the east it merges into the built-up area of London, and in the south its boundary runs across the middle of Heathrow Airport. Nor is Hillingdon a clear-cut labour market. At the Census of 1981 just over half the employed men and 37 per cent of the employed women living in Hillingdon worked outside the borough – most so in the case of managers and professionals – and there is a corresponding inflow from other areas into Hillingdon. As a manager said: one of my local directors lives in Camberley, another in Princes Risborough, and I live in Weybridge. There are better public transport links eastwards to Central London than from North to South within the borough: and, while easy access to Central London is in many ways an advantage, it can also be a disadvantage when, for example, there is a question of attracting support for local professional associations.

Socially, Hillingdon is heterogeneous, with a marked North-South divide: residential and Conservative to the north, industrial and Labour in the south. Swindon and Sheffield, of course, are also socially heterogeneous, but in their case heterogeneity is contained within the unity of a well-defined city.

Moreover, there has not been the same pressure in Hillingdon as in the other two cities for people and organisations to pull together to promote the area's development, for the borough has had neither the planned and dramatic expansion of Swindon nor Sheffield's problems of unemployment and the decline of traditional industries.

The question we have asked about Hillingdon is, therefore: what happens to companies' community involvement and its promotion in an area where civic unity is still in the process of being created and the pressure for action to solve the community's problems is relatively low?

A prosperous community

Hillingdon has been and is economically prosperous. It is served by the M4, the M40, and the M25, is well placed at the end of the M4 high-technology corridor, and has benefited from the nearness and expansion of Heathrow. The locally employed work force in 1986 was 123,000. Unemployment has been consistently below the London average. It rose to 6.4 per cent in 1984, but fell to 2.2 per cent by January 1990. The borough has a substantial manufacturing sector. Manufacturing jobs were lost in the 1970s and early 1980s, but in 1984 manufacturing still provided 22 per cent of local jobs, compared to 17 per cent in London as a whole. There have been major recent increases in office employment, notably in Uxbridge and on the new Stockley Park estate near Heathrow, which has attracted an impressive array of high-technology firms or subsidiaries. It is still, however, male manual workers who tend to do particularly well in Hillingdon. The New Earnings Survey of 1989 showed that they made up a higher proportion of the full-time work force in the borough than in London as a whole and had higher earnings, whereas, in spite of the increase in office employment, women not only hold a markedly lower proportion of local jobs than in London as a whole but earn 10 per cent below the London average.

Growth in local employment continues. The borough's forecast is that between 1987 and 2001 the net increase in industrial and office employment might be of the order of 9,000 to 12,500. Add likely increases in retailing, leisure and recreation, and hotels, notably around Heathrow, and the total is well above the expected increase of 4,700 to 8,800 in the number of economically active residents.

Problems which remain

Prosperity has not, of course, done away with the range of social problems and opportunities which exist in any community, like service to old people, the disabled, and the mentally handicapped, or the need to develop youth work or the arts. In the area of social service alone, the Hillingdon Partnership Trust (below) has no difficulty in compiling and up-dating a list of problems to whose solution business might be, and is, asked to contribute. On the economic side, a borough report in 1989 notes that it is no longer so necessary 'to stimulate employment opportunities and to promote Hillingdon as a business location', but (summarising a long list of recommendations) that problems of four main kinds still need to be targeted, and again with the suggestion that in all these areas business could help.

Targeted recruitment

At the end of 1989 only one ward in Hillingdon had over 4 per cent unemployment, but there were still pockets of long-term unemployment in some of the older industrial areas, chiefly among older workers without the skills needed in the new office and high-technology establishments. Other needs noted are for better opportunities for disabled workers, for women returners, including employer-provided creches, and for ethnic minority groups.

Local recruitment: maintainance of the environment

These two issues are linked. 'Enhancing the quality/attractiveness of the environment of employment areas' is noted as an issue in its own right, but also connects to that of local recruitment by way of problems of traffic congestion. Hillingdon residents have benefited from access to the wider London labour market, but, as cross-flows of traffic develop, the borough is beginning to choke up. Already by 1981 three out of five men and two out of five women commuted to work by car. Since then the traffic has thickened, and industrial informants commented sharply on the difficulties which this is beginning to cause. There are only limited possibilities of reducing the pressure by new road building or improvements in public transport within the borough. Why not, one informant asked, extend the Underground south from Uxbridge to make a circle through Heathrow? –

but more in hope than in expectation. The borough's report suggests, however, that much might be done to reduce commuting and other traffic through 'pursuit of measures to reduce the need for high volume and long distance': for example local hiring and purchasing, or gearing training policies to mismatches between the skills of the resident population and those required by local employers, or housing policies (including a 'promotional role with key employers') targeted to reduce inward commuting.

Low-cost premises
One result of the influx of large companies able to afford substantial rents – though at least one of these has moved out again because of recent rent increases – has been to create a shortage of premises at affordable costs for small or start-up firms, and also for social organisations. A desk space near the civic centre, as one voluntary social service officer commented, may now cost £100 a week, and a number of voluntary associations are now either severely cramped for space or without accommodation altogether.

Raising the quality of performance of smaller firms
'Many middle-sized firms could do better' if they could be reached with business advice or helped through local purchasing. Efforts are being made, as one informant said, 'but they are hard to get at'.

Action on these problems

'It's the Hillingdon style: everyone does his own thing'.
[Comment by a borough officer]

A great deal, actually, gets done in Hillingdon, and not least by companies. On economic and planning problems, 'if large local firms are asked, they will help', and banks and professional partnerships are a useful source of contacts when trying to raise the quality of performance in smaller firms. The local enterprise agency, HILENTA, which specialises in small business start-ups and advice, was set up by small businesses themselves, and now has the backing of banks and other major businesses. The Hillingdon Partnership Trust has been able to 'broker' substantial donations from large firms into local social service projects. Some at least of the large businesses which have moved into Hillingdon have or are setting up regular community relations policies which benefit local as well as other causes. Not all do so, of course: the J-shaped curve noted in our Swindon case study applies here as well. Informants note, without being too specific, the 'cosy relationship' which exists between a number of companies, large or small, and individual social service establishments or associations. The 17 Rotaries, Inner Wheels, Lions Clubs, and Round Tables make their expected contribution to social causes ('It's their job', as one outside informant said): modest in each case, but adding to a significant total. School-business links are well developed, in Hillingdon as elsewhere, and the important linkages which are beginning to form round Brunel University are described below.

All this, however, is happening in a scattered and piecemeal way, often on a rather modest scale. Nothing in our interviews suggests that Hillingdon companies, taken individually, are different from companies elsewhere either in their willingness to become involved in the community or in their procedures for doing so. What is under-developed in Hillingdon is the network of influences which could make the culture of giving in the borough more coherent and drive its development faster. There are centres and networks of influence with at least the potential to do this, but their development has a very long way to go.

'There are no business mafias', one informant after another agreed, unless the Hillingdon Partnership Trust is counted as one: though, as will be seen, there are interesting possibilities for the future. A manager in one large company with significant local involvement said nevertheless that 'I work in isolation'. Nor is there any obvious lead company like Allied Dunbar in Swindon. Hillingdon has its share of companies in good standing in Business in the Community or the Per Cent Club, but we found no sign of these national organisations reaching into the borough to dynamise and coordinate local efforts. BitC has a North-West London Business Leadership Team, but its area extends only as far as Ealing.

The Hillingdon Partnership Trust makes a major contribution to 'federated giving' in the social services, but still with restrictions which the voluntary social service sector finds irritating, and the Hillingdon Association of Voluntary Services is too understaffed even to keep in touch with the whole range of voluntary associations in the borough, let alone to campaign for business support. In the arts, as in some areas of social service (old people's welfare, in particular) efforts to overcome the traditional division between small-scale activities in the old districts began to show results only in 1988/9.

Even in the borough, there has been a tendency for departments or sections of departments to go their own way, partly through lack of strong political leadership. In May 1990 the borough council came under one-party

(Conservative) control, but for some years previously it was hung. Informants agreed that, by contrast with some other councils in the same position, the three parties did not work together well enough to provide effective leadership or get new departures through.

If, then, one was looking for a more coordinated and cohesive effort to assess and act on Hillingdon's problems, and in that context to market community involvement more effectively to the companies operating there, where would be the points at which to take hold?

Social welfare: the Hillingdon Partnership Trust and the voluntary social services
The Hillingdon Partnership Trust (HPT)
The HPT is the major success story of marketing the 'culture of giving' in Hillingdon – and yet with certain reservations. In 1980 a large local firm wanted to help disadvantaged people, and agreed to contribute £25,000 for an intermediate treatment centre which the borough had been unable to finance. The idea of thus 'brokering' business money into social services, the borough's Social Services Department thought, could with advantage be applied elsewhere, and so the Partnership was formed. Its current board includes three members from business, one of whom is chairman, two officers from Social Services, one borough councillor, and two local MPs. Its charter is to improve and enrich the lives of disadvantaged people within Hillingdon Borough, with a strong qualification that the aim is to 'add the icing to the cake', not to replace public services or fill gaps in them.

In a first experimental period HPT is said to have 'bumbled along': it was not, for example, at first registered as a charity, so that giving through it was not tax-efficient. By the second half of the 1980s, however, its business management was tightened and its sights were raised: 'tugging business people's hearts properly', as it was put, rather than let them 'tug their hearts out for small items'. Discussion with an outside consultant with wide business contacts led to agreement to target the larger local firms at national chief executive level: to 'go from the top down, the only proven method'. A previous attempt at cold canvassing with the help of a retired marketing manager had given little result. Now a more direct and personal approach was tried: two dinners at the House of Commons (a drink, a short speech by the chairman, then 'buttonhole them over the meal') were followed up through visits to individual companies, and with success. 'HPT needs legs': a full time officer was assigned by the borough in 1985, and one result of the new contacts was a secondment from British Rail, with a view particularly to getting out and about among medium and smaller firms.

The borough's Social Services department keeps HPT in touch with social service problems and opportunities, and the borough also advises HPT of new firms coming in so that it can contact them as they arrive. Where a problem is identified, HPT 'hunts' for a company to solve it, according to where individual companies' interests lie. It may ask for cash, but more often asks for for commitments of time, energy, and skills from volunteers at all levels ('are you interested in helping to put in this machine?'), or for equipment such as computers for disabled people. In any case it asks for project rather than continuing support. Its appeal is to a mixture of altruism and self-interest. 'We know how to tweak people's conscience, and they do have a conscience', but that does not exclude public relations through HPT's brochures or otherwise. Pensioners, it was said, liked to see the Penguin logo on the Age Concern directory for which the company paid. There were some revealing comments on how business participants' own attitudes changed as they became more personally involved in HPT projects: exhilarating and widening, one said, or 'it became a personal crusade'.

We have had a blow by blow account from more than one participant of how one substantial project, the building and adaptation of a canal narrow boat for use by disabled people at a cost of £60,000, was pursued through successive stages with the management of the Stockley Park estate and its tenant firms: 'our clearest example of how to make things happen'. 'Someone has to make things happen', and the HPT does. By 1990 it could claim to have raised nearly half a million pounds in cash and kind, £300,000 within the previous three years.

In spite of these successes, outside informants were ambivalent in their views of HPT. Valuable, certainly, in its own field, and very useful to firms which can cope with the flood of appeals by saying that they give through HPT. But is that field wide enough? Health, environmental, and many educational projects, other than for children with disabilities, are not within HPT's terms of reference. A business informant would have preferred HPT to be a general agency for federated giving on the lines of the American United Way. Social service informants wondered whether HPT overemphasised causes close to the Social Services Department, though this may be changing: one reason why HPT took up an offer from RAF Uxbridge to provide office space for their secondee was a wish to move HPT more 'out of the borough'. Or should HPT go more for cash, which charities need, as distinct from gifts in kind? And is HPT, as some suggested, a barrier as well as an opportunity? Once companies were committed to HPT, it was said, approaches by voluntary associations even outside HPT's field become more difficult.

The voluntary social services: a campaigning approach?

One answer to the latter problem could be joint campaigning by voluntary associations themselves, complementary to the work of HPT. Informants outside as well as in management recognised the irritation to companies of a stream of uncoordinated appeals: federated giving through HPT was a convenience even to large companies, and even more, as a community relations manager in one of them said, to smaller companies which do not in any case have the staff and time to process appeals properly. Time pressures in companies with slimmed-down staffs were stressed in several interviews. 'We arrive at 8 and leave at 6.30', as one manager said, and anyway 'none of us lives here'. Social service informants recognised that companies might reasonably have their doubts about allowing individual voluntary associations access to company premises for fund-raising or recruiting volunteers.

There has been occasional joint campaigning, for example a week's display at the Civic Centre two years ago to promote GAYE ('relieving people of standing on street corners rattling tins'). This had little result: a scheme was started among borough staff, but approaches to companies did not take off. Hopes that employee 'moles' might put pressure on their companies were not realised. In another case, however, operating on the employee network did pay off. Employees of one company ran a successful fund-raising drive, matched £ for £ by the company ('and had fun – important!'). They then became more ambitious, and got together with the Association for Voluntary Service to find others to share with them.

But there have been two difficulties in the way of joint campaigning by voluntary associations on any larger or more systematic scale. One is the persistence of the old divisions in the borough. Age Concern came into Hillingdon, with a decidedly entrepreneurial role, only in 1989, when the four previous old people's welfare committees were at last persuaded to recognise that, with the rising number of old people, the level of service required was beyond them and that they needed the back-up of a major national agency.

The other difficulty, and the main one, is lack of resources for campaigning. The staff of the Hillingdon Association of Voluntary Services is a general secretary and a clerical assistant. The AVS, as was said above, cannot even keep adequately in touch with the voluntary associations in the borough: 200 in AVS membership, perhaps two or three hundred more 'out there', if not more: but an extra staff member would be needed to research the field. 'What we need is more resources to mount a campaign'. Our interviewer suggested contacting ARC for a possible secondment. Less cramped accommodation would also help, if the voluntary associations could afford it. One company offered the whole top floor of its large new building, in a first-class location: but it was offered as a shell, and the voluntary associations could not afford to adapt and equip it.

There is, it was said, a national angle to the question of campaigning. National bodies like NCVO needed to do a better public relations job to correct the image of voluntary service as amateur and low-level, concerned with flag days and cups of tea: 'the wrong idea of volunteering for Hillingdon'. But the important thing was more money and staff to market voluntary social services locally, and without necessarily expecting associations' national headquarters to provide it. Some local people were said to be disillusioned because they had expected Age Concern to bring a lot of money with them: they had not realised that it must be locally and, as it happens, somewhat uncertainly, financed.

A Hillingdon Community Trust – or is HPT one already?

So, how might collective marketing by the social service organisations be better systematised and resourced?

HPT is a community trust within CAF's definition, and CAF recognises it as such. The Hillingdon Association for Voluntary Service considered at one point taking steps to establish a community trust of its own, but dropped the idea because the Partnership 'were there first – and it is hard to talk to them'. HPT, however is a community trust of a special kind, at one extreme of the spectrum of CTs, since in principle it passes all its receipts through and does not accumulate an endowment: whereas, as is shown in Paper II, CAF's preferred model for the time being is the endowed trust on American lines. The range of causes which HPT serves is also limited, as has been shown.

What would appear to be needed on the side of the social services in Hillingdon – over and above the efforts of individual agencies – is a well-focussed and high-profile system of campaigning for a wider range of causes than that served by HPT, with provision built in for development work and for types of funding not always forthcoming from year-to-year appeals: like core as distinct from project funding, or capital grants for accommodation, or meeting the emergencies which may arise when the flow of funds to individual agencies varies. There is a good case for having both, as the manager quoted above argued, an association to organise federated giving over the whole range of charitable causes, on the lines of the United Way, and a community trust with a substantial endowment and the functions described in Papers II and III. The two could be combined under one name and roof, a modified and extended version of HPT, or they could, following American practice, operate complementarily alongside each other. Hillingdon needs a decision to take one or other of these paths.

Business networks

With the important but limited exception of HPT, Hillingdon does not have business 'mafias' like the Swindon Partnership, engaged in discussing issues of community involvement and in drawing companies into the net. But there are local networks of which use could be, and to an extent is, made for developing the culture of giving, and at least one of these could be of major importance.

HILENTA and the Economic Development Unit

There is the germ of one such network in HILENTA, the local enterprise agency, and the borough's Economic Development Unit, which is also concerned, as was said above, with improving the quality of performance of smaller local firms. Both do useful work. HILENTA specialises in advice for new-start and existing small businesses, and in 1989 helped the creation of between ninety and a hundred new small businesses. The Economic Development Unit promotes a range of activities including training days, Meet Local Buyers seminars, and perhaps in future a Made in Hillingdon exhibition. The EDU has its own network of business contacts. HILENTA is supported and financed mainly by business: the rest of its budget comes from training fees and a Department of Employment grant which will run out in 1991. It works particularly directly with the banks, advising clients referred from them and training junior bank managers in small business advisory work.

Both agencies, however, are small-scale and low profile. I was startled, one informant said, to see the small scale of the EDU after what I was used to in Cleveland. HILENTA operates with three part-time staff (but a secondee from British Rail has just been added) out of a partly converted flat over a shop well away from the borough's main centres, with a very modest budget of £23,500, and even this budget is somewhat uncertain. Company supporters were said to be adopting a more business-like approach: 'good community people' it was said, appreciating that they had an obligation to help in promoting new businesses, but there was point in the observation that a number were shifting their contribution to the enterprise agency from their charitable to their marketing budget. Though, however, business subscriptions continue to flow in on a modest scale, averaging about £750 per firm, HILENTA like many other receivers of business grants is finding it harder than a few years ago to get firm commitments to funding beyond one year. New sponsors are still being obtained, mainly through personal connections and approaches to larger firms, but lack of time and staff has made it difficult to extend HILENTA's appeal more widely. The new BR secondee, however, will be expected to work with his BR colleague seconded to HPT to reach a new range of firms.

Moreover, HILENTA and the EDU are not only geographically separate but somewhat at arm's length. Unusually for an enterprise agency, HILENTA has no grant or other support from the borough. The question of a 'one-stop' business advisory centre like the Great Western Business Centre at Swindon has not been raised, but, if it were, it was questioned whether HILENTA's business supporters would welcome a move which might identify it too much with the borough. It was noted that in other neighbouring boroughs there has been less reluctance of this kind: Harrow, for example, has brought its enterprise agency into a prominent new block where its work can have a higher profile. To an outside observer, there is little question that Hillingdon also needs to move towards a more visible and better resourced business-local authority partnership for small and medium enterprise development.

Localised business networks
One localised network is among firms on the new Stockley Park estate, where the estate management is itself interested in community involvement, and the social and sports facilities on the estate provide an occasion for managers and staff to get together. These firms' attitudes were said to vary along the usual J-shaped curve: some interested, but a good deal of apathy, and in any case depending often on local personalities. The fact that some of them are 'blue chip' companies was said for some local purposes to be a disadvantage. National policies and procedures for community relations might or might not accommodate local projects. As Age Concern was told by a company elsewhere in Hillingdon, 'We support Age Concern *nationally*' – not least, as that company told us, through a successful GAYE scheme with £ for £ matching company grants. Companies' national procedures could also be rigid in other respects, like long advance notice of projects if they were to catch the company budget.

Nevertheless, some at least of the Stockley Park companies have become involved through the localised network, either in their corporate capacity or through the spread of employee initiatives from one company to another. It is a 'drip feed problem', it was said, a question of passing the word in a variety of areas and ways, and remembering that companies tend to prefer projects like that for the narrow boat with which they can identify and by identified. The estate at least provides an environment in which 'drip feed' is possible.

So also tenants of the new Pavilions shopping centre in Uxbridge were said to work together and, among other things, to cooperate with the voluntary social services: stalls for publicity for charities, a fashion show with the proceeds going to charity, and approaches have been made to interest them in Give As You Earn.

Potentially there could be a number of other localised networks on the industrial estates, round the airport, or in the main office and shopping areas. A further possibility might be more positive and cohesive action by the five Chambers of Commerce and Trade (as one informant exclaimed,' FIVE Chambers!'). The Chambers may assist to some extent with, for example, contacts for school-business links, but in principle do not at present involve themselves with charitable giving: favouring one cause, it was said, means disfavouring another. There might, it was said, be a whip-round at the annual dinner: 'when they've had a few, they pay up'.

Leadership from the university? The Brunel factor
The most potentially significant business network, however, is centred at Brunel University, and there could also be interesting possibilities of community leadership from the university as such.

Brunel has in any case a wide range of local as well as national business contacts through its research services, and a wide range of contacts through its network of local placements for students on sandwich courses. It has also, as part of its programme for marketing itself to industry, established a Chief Executives' Club, a general discussion group for senior managers with ninety to a hundred organisations in membership, eight meetings a year, and a usual attendance of around fifteen. Lively, it was said, and easy to recruit for it, but not very clear in its objectives. Brunel has therefore gone on to establish a Brunel Business Partnership, with a full-time administrator, to link firms more clearly to the university. Firms pay a substantial subscription for access both to academic services like seminars and libraries and to the university's sports and arts facilities. A local company gave a substantial start-up grant.

The club and the BBP have been created primarily for the university's own purposes. Whereas, it was said, many businesses some years ago wanted an association with higher education, but could not see the way in, there are now so many ways in that business 'does not know where to start'. Clearly, however, these associations are networks of which use could be made in developing the local 'culture of giving', perhaps with repercussions into the university's own teaching and research. Paper II notes the case for an academic or 'quasi-academic' contribution to systematising the theory and ideology of corporate community involvement and building it into the main stream of business thinking and particularly of management education. At present Brunel's management teaching and research do not reach into that area.

Brunel reaches out into the community in a number of other ways besides its business contacts. The public comes to its concerts and uses its sports facilities; the university reaches all local secondary schools through its education liaison staff; an increasing proportion of its students are local and living at home. It has not hitherto taken a leading local role of the kind common in American civic universities, partly because of attitudes in the university itself and partly, it was suggested, because even after the university's more than twenty years in the borough the community is not quite sure what use to make of it. But there was a strong suggestion that this might be changing, in much the same way as might happen with any other large business. The analogy with a large business is a good one, for Brunel does in fact see itself in that way. There are signs of more awareness of the university's responsibility in and to the community and of the benefits which could follow for Brunel as, it was suggested, they have for other universities. Staff shortages have made development in that direction difficult, but relevant new appointments are on the way.

The borough

Hillingdon Borough Council's reputation for lack of leadership or, as one informant said, of marketing orientation, and for inability to get new things done, is not wholly deserved. Actually the borough has led and is leading in a number of fields relevant to the culture of corporate giving.

The Hillingdon Partnership Trust, after all, was created by and still has administrative support from the borough's Social Services Department. There was no corporate plan for economic development, but by 1989 the borough was shaping one in the context of its statutory duties to prepare a Unitary Development Plan and an economic development strategy. '*Chief Officers are concerned to ensure a corporate approach* to the economic development strategy, since at least eight of its departments are concerned': the italics are those of the borough officers. The indications quoted earlier of possible objectives and private sector involvement are taken from the borough's papers.

In the arts, the borough has taken the lead in persuading the four local arts associations to work together under the umbrella of the Hillingdon Arts Association, and through an Arts Forum which brings the Association together with borough councillors and staff. 'A nightmare', as one officer said, but it has been done. The Forum met for the first time in November 1989 to adopt a general policy for the arts in the borough, with the accent in the first place on public finance from the borough itself and from Greater London Arts, but an eye also to partnerships where 'a relatively small amount of public money can attract funds from... industry, commerce, trusts and individual donors'.

Organisation to promote school-business links was described as 'less sophisticated' in Hillingdon than over the border in Buckinghamshire, which has like Wiltshire (Paper III) an industry-education liaison committee, whereas Hillingdon has not. Figures on the extent of work experience placements, teacher secondments, and so on were not easily to hand: they were, certainly, on the computer, but 'computers are all over the department'. 'Hillingdon has never got over being a borough', and even within the borough structure the old administrative divisions still persist. Nevertheless, in Hillingdon as elsewhere the promotion of school-business links has been extensive and successful. Companies' attitudes are seen as positive. Schools, as elsewhere, 'own' their links with business, and use their own parental and local networks to recruit governors or set up work experience or careers visits. Borough staff have put in hard work over a number of years to help them to do so. As a Chamber of Commerce informant respectfully noted: we may put an advertisement for work experience placings in our newsletter, but the borough's careers staff go round to 'every shop'. 'It's the job people's job', and they do it.

The administration of training policies is more coordinated, through a consortium from the relevant sections within the Education Department ('a good model which ought to be followed'), and there is an interesting initiative in relation to the Training and Enterprise Council. The TEC for Hillingdon also covers Hounslow, Richmond, and Ealing, and the borough is not represented on it. But there is a proposal to bring together local industrialists with the borough officers dealing with TVEI, employment and youth training in a 'mini-TEC' to define Hillingdon's needs and process them through the wider official TEC.

Links with companies on youth work, like school-business links, are a case of progress in spite of fragmentation. The Education Department has half a dozen link/liaison officers scattered through the department: not helpful, it was pointed out, since the approach to companies which works tends to be person-to-person, by a particular link/liaison officer to a particular known manager, at or near the top. It is only recently that a single Assistant Director has been given overall responsibility for this area. Nevertheless, much cooperation has been achieved. In the area of youth/community work as in that of school-business links companies are seen as forthcoming. Most large local companies are thought to be involved, often through personal relationships, with or without any intervention by borough staff. Self-interest, as usual, plays its part as well as altruism. Stockley Park tenants were irritated by motor-cyclists riding round the estate, and worked with the borough to convert a piece of off-site land. One of Grand Metropolitan's aims in backing a a non-alcoholic bar for young people was to offset the alcoholic image of some parts of its business. The main reservation about companies' contribution is that they tend to give most easily for projects – the typical formula was said to be either a small cash gift, or else actual involvement in a project – and the borough has had little success in securing core or staff funding.

There is truth in outsiders' unfavourable comments about lack of leadership from the borough. There are illustrations in the notes above about the Economic Development Unit and HILENTA, or failure to appreciate the potential of Brunel, or confusion in some respects over the role of the Hillingdon Partnership Trust. It is true that borough administration has been fragmented and that in a number of ways the borough has been 'not market-oriented'. But what has been achieved should not be under-estimated: divisions between and within departments are beginning to be bridged; and the return to one-party control may ensure stronger political leadership, though this, especially in the context of charge-capping, remains to be seen. There is the potential for a stronger and more coherent lead from the borough in future.

Conclusion

Hillingdon, where the culture of giving is concerned, is not a desert, but it is only patchily cultivated land. There are points from which to build a stronger local promotional effort, but who is to build it? Some development could and probably will follow on from existing initiatives. The borough, as the one clearly central and unifying agency in Hillingdon, could certainly have a key role in building new partnerships with business. So might

119

Brunel, and so might the HPT in collaboration with the voluntary social service sector. But, in the end, the impression is that in at least three ways progress could be accelerated by new action from outside.

- If Hillingdon is a town still looking for an identity, and with neither the obvious unity nor the obvious pressures for common action found in Swindon or Sheffield, then it is a natural candidate for a Common Purpose community leadership training programme, to create among future leaders in the community a common view of the problems of the community and its various sectors and a habit of talking to each other about them across sectoral boundaries.

- BitC Business Leadership Teams have not been concerned with areas like Hillingdon: but they should be. The problems in Hillingdon to which business might contribute may not be as glaringly obvious as elsewhere in North-East London or in a city like Sheffield, but they are real and large, and include not only problems of social welfare such as those for which the HPT was created but those identified in the borough's reports on economic development and management of the environment, which fit directly into categories with which BitC's Target Teams have been concerned. Another possibility might be a business-led initiative from the area TEC, with a contribution from the suggested local 'mini-TEC'. One way or the other, Hillingdon could be fruitful ground for a major business-led initiative from outside.

- There could with advantage be a similar initiative by CAF, with or without participation by other bodies such as NCVO, to sort out the issues raised above about the role and resourcing of HPT, joint campaigning by the voluntary sector associations, and a possible endowed community trust. Federated giving has developed in Hillingdon in a significant way, but needs to be put on a more permanent and comprehensive basis, United Way style; and an endowed community trust is still a dream for the future.

VI Learning From America

Compared to companies in Britain, companies in America invest in their communities very generously indeed. The median for declared donations by companies in Britain (Paper I) is between 0.1 and 0.2 per cent of pre-tax profits. Even if this proportion is doubled, or more, to allow for under-declaration and for other forms of 'community involvement', it is still far behind the average for all companies in the United States. At the end of the 1980s this was 1.8 per cent for tax-deductible contributions, or 2-2.5 per cent when other 'corporate assistance' expenditure is added.

American experience can be looked at in either of two ways. One is to look at particular initiatives pioneered in America, like Per Cent Clubs, community trusts, community leadership progammes, federated giving, or styles of management of the 'contributions function', and to consider whether to adopt them in Britain. As previous papers have shown, that is happening already, and increasingly so in the last few years. The other is to examine the process by which the culture of giving has been developed in America and ask what lessons this might have for developing it in Britain. The process of promoting community investment by companies is the central theme of this report, and we therefore take the second approach.

From this point of view, American experience has three themes.

- It underlines the need to approach companies in terms of their individual circumstances and interests. Companies' contributions can be averaged to find a general trend, but every company is an individual case: in terms of marketing, an individual customer.

- It shows that building a culture of giving is a long haul, but also how in the right conditions its growth can be sharply accelerated.

- The right conditions include national policies on the respective roles of government and the private sector, on the law on company giving, and on taxation and incentives; but building a culture of giving depends first and foremost on personal initiatives and contacts through informal or formal networks.

Every company is an individual case

It is important not to be bemused by American averages. The first lesson about corporate giving in America is that it has no standard pattern. Averages for corporate giving are derived from a very wide scatter indeed. There are in America broad influences on the 'culture of giving' which operate across the economy, and conventions about 'best practice' which companies may or may not choose to adopt. But there is in the end no standardisation of the amounts which individual companies invest in their communities, the causes they support, or the ways in which they manage their investment: individuality and diversity are the norm. One reason is that in America as in Britain some companies lag behind the best practice of others in similar circumstances. But the principal reason is simply that companies' circumstances, interests, and potential differ. In America as in Britain every company is an individual case, and the message about corporate investment in the community has to be tailored to that company in its individual situation in the market and community.

The 1989 edition of the United States Conference Board's annual *Survey of Corporate Contributions* was based on replies to a questionnaire by 328 out of 1,200 'top' US firms, with a strong bias to the largest. Even within this limited universe, let alone what might be found from examining firms outside it, patterns of giving were very diversified indeed.

The median charitable (tax-deductible) contribution by companies in the sample was 1.05 per cent of US pre-tax income, but the lower quartile was 0.56 per cent and the upper quartile 2.03 per cent, and this spread had not changed significantly since 1978. Some companies returned percentages of 6, 8, and 10 per cent, but another American report, looking beyond the Conference Board sample, comments that 'the typical American company does not give at all', because it is likely still to be struggling for growth and profitability, and will become a 'giver' only when it reaches a 'plateau of profitability'. The Conference Board sample showed differences between broad industrial categories, with manufacturing and insurance companies giving on the average three times as high a percentage of pre-tax profits as those in utilities and telecommunications: between industries within these categories (0.53 per cent, for example, for paper and paper products, but 2.66 per cent for 'other manufacturing'); and, especially, a spread in every category from companies giving 0.25 per cent or less to others giving 4 per cent or more.

Size, measured by assets in the US or the amount of US profits, made little difference to the median percentage contribution over most of the size distribution, though as a percentage of pre-tax profits the smallest companies tended to give most. But in every size bracket there was a spread of between three and five to one between the most and the least generous givers.

Sharp year to year variations were noted, with only a very general relationship to changes in pre-tax profits. In 1989 companies in the catch-all category of 'business services' expected to increase their contributions budget in the next year by an average of one third, whereas electrical machinery and equipment companies intended to reduce theirs by nearly a quarter: so cancelling an increase of one third in the previous year, when, by contrast, printing and publishing companies had cut their contributions by nearly 40 per cent.

Tax-deductible contributions in the United States include the cost of certain types of giving in kind – securities, company products, property, equipment – and this again varied widely. Among the 75 largest corporate donors in the sample, measured by the absolute size of donation, 31 gave only cash, but 11 made half or more of their donations in non-cash forms. Classifying by industries, there was little of this sort of giving in banking, finance, distribution, utilities, or oil and gas, but much more in manufacturing: companies in electrical machinery and equipment made over two-fifths of their donations in these forms.

Companies also provide 'corporate assistance', which is not tax-deductible: grants to colleges and universities for basic research, support for public radio and television, support for other non-profit organisations through subscriptions, secondments, gifts of product and property, 'soft' loans, or free use of office space or services: and for the Conference Board's purposes 'corporate assistance' also includes the costs of administering companies' 'contributions function'. Altogether, corporate assistance is estimated to have accounted between 1983 and 1987 for about 20 per cent of what companies gave. Many companies in the Conference Board sample found it hard to estimate their corporate assistance expenditure, but among those who could there was again wide variation. Industry averages ranged from 5 per cent of total giving up to, in banking, 22 per cent.

The destination of corporate contributions also varied. There were broad tendencies from year to year across all sampled companies, for example a progressive fall in the percentage of contributions going to health and welfare services and a related fall in 'federated giving', which is largely for these services. But again, there were wide differences within the general trend. Transport and utility companies gave a particularly high proportion of their contributions to health and welfare, and passed a correspondingly high proportion of them through federated giving. Non-manufacturing companies passed twice as many dollars per employee through federated giving as manufacturers. Chemical, oil and gas, and electrical machinery companies gave on the average over 40 per cent of their contributions to education, whereas the range in most non-manufacturing industries was 18 to 28 per cent.

Companies' ways of managing their contributions function were examined in a 1982 Conference Board report on *The Corporate Contributions Function*, and again the variety of styles stood out. The largest corporations were likely to have a structured and professionally staffed programme, but this faded even among substantial companies into 'semi-structured' programmes with part-time staffing, and on down into 'informal structure that does not fit into the questionnaire format'. This was not necessarily, the report noted, a difference between good and bad practice: there could, for example, be advantages for a contributions officer in having other duties which create regular contacts with colleagues in other departments. Companies might or might not set up their own foundations alongside a direct giving programme: the largest givers had usually done so, smaller givers usually not, but there was no standard rule. Where in a company the contributions function was situated and to whom its staff reported differed, and this function might not include all the activities which might be expected. United Way campaigns, for example, were more likely to be administered by personnel. In most industries most of the contributions budget was spent by company HQs, but within each industry the proportion spent in the field varied from company to company anywhere within the range from 0 to over 90 per cent.

There are other variations, for instance in company support for programmes for volunteering from the workplace[1] or for community leadership programmes.[2] But there is no need to labour the point further. Whatever average trends there may be, and whether one looks at the level

---

1   K.K. Allen, I. Chapin, S. Keller, and D. Hill, *Volunteers from the Workplace, National Center for Voluntary Action*, Washington DC, 1979: C. Vizza, K. Allen, and S. Keller, *A New Competitive Edge*, Volunteer – the National Center, Washington DC, 1986.

2   C.M. Moore (ed.), *A Colorful Quilt*, NACLO, Indianapolis, 1988.

of contributions, their destination, or their management, American companies' community investment policies are individual and diversity is the norm.

Diversity becomes still more obvious when the picture is enlarged to include the way in which American companies operate outside the United States. Next door, in Canada, they find themselves in a culture where average giving by a sample of companies in 1985 and 1986 was 0.4-0.5 per cent of pre-tax profits,[3] well below the level in the USA. Our own interviews have thrown up illustrations of the variety of American companies' practice in Britain and Europe. In one family-owned company, the family insists that practice in the USA shall be reflected world-wide, and its British subsidiary is by British standards an exceptionally generous giver. Another American company distinguishes between its markets. One of its divisions in Britain has a high consumer profile, and this division is a large giver; but another produces basic materials, with no final consumer contact, and its management has had to argue hard with corporate headquarters to justify a much smaller budget, even though its operations have nuisance value and good local relationships are a matter of urgency. A third company explained how differences between the communities in which it operates in Britain, France, and Germany and in its status as an employer in local labour markets had led it to adopt very different community relations policies in the three countries, and to switch its policy in Germany from the French to the British model when it moved its German plant to a new location.

A long haul, but it can be accelerated

The second lesson from America is an ambiguous one, discouraging yet at the same time promising. It is that building American companies' 'culture of giving' has been a long haul, over several decades: but the good news is that its development can be, and in certain periods like the 1980s has been, speeded up sharply if the circumstances are right. Britain, of course, can in any case benefit from following in the footsteps of American pioneers, and is doing so, as previous papers have shown. The lesson from America itself is that the speed at which companies learn depends on circumstances, and when the right circumstances are created it can be fast.

In some areas of American corporate giving the main and most rapid phase of development lies back in the past, and this is particularly true of

3   *Corporate Giving in Canada 1986*, Institute of Donations and Public Affairs Research, Montreal.

the United Way, whose main growth occurred at a time when corporate giving in Britain was under-developed. Whereas more recent American developments have been quickly picked up in Britain, the United Way was not: 'federated giving' by corporations and their employees, mainly through United Ways, with associated involvement of volunteers and secondees, has been and remains a more important feature of the American than of the British scene. The United Way began at Denver in 1887, borrowing from a model developed in Liverpool ten years earlier. In 1920, however, there were still only 61 United Ways – not even, at that time, with a common name – which raised $23 million: not all, of course, from companies or from employees as such. Then takeoff began. There were 450 United Ways by the early 1930s, 800 by the end of the second World War, and since the 1950s the number has plateaued around 2,200. By the mid-1970s the amount raised each year passed $1 billion. At first collections tended to be 'mostly from the wealthy', but payroll deductions were introduced in 1943, and the accent has shifted towards employee giving. The current working of local United Ways is shown in the appendix to this paper.

The last fifteen years, however, and especially the 1980s, have been a time of generally accelerated development in corporate giving, in the first place in its overall level. Table 4.1 shows that just before the second World War tax-deductible contributions by American companies averaged 0.45 per cent of pre-tax profits. Giving rose to around 0.75 per cent in the war years, and then plateaued from the 1950s through the 1970s at 0.9-1.0 per cent. From there onwards, however, it took off sharply to reach 1.8 per cent at the end of the 1980s, and the new level of giving was quickly consolidated. A Presidential task force on private sector initiatives, appointed at the end of 1981, recommended that a reasonable minimum for company giving should be two per cent of pre-tax profits. Per Cent Clubs had already been invented – a Five Per Cent club, for example, was formed at Minneapolis in 1976 – and now they spread rapidly. By 1988 there were around 750 clubs with members committed to give 2, 5, and even in one case 10 per cent.

A feature of United Ways has always been support from within companies by volunteers and secondees, but this is something different from company-organised volunteering from the workplace for more general purposes. In this area too there has been a rapid recent take-off. In the mid 1970s it was reported that 'employee volunteer programs in most companies are not taken seriously, are given relatively low priority, and do not have the resources needed to be successful'. By 1986, however, 'Over the last ten years corporations have become one of the primary sources of

Table 4.1   Charitable (tax-deductible) contributions by US corporations as a percentage
of pre-tax profits

Per cent

1936-40	0.45
1941-50	0.74
1951-60	0.92
1961-70	1.07
1971-80	0.93
1981-85	1.65
1986 & 1987	1.81

US Department of Commerce, Internal Revenue Service

volunteers for non-profit organisations', with programmes in both large and small companies in all sectors, and a significant contribution from the trade unions: what the Vizza/Allen study just quoted headlines as 'Volunteering – Organised Labor's Best Kept Secret'.

United Ways raise money primarily for current revenue support, but the United States also has several hundred endowed community foundations, which build a capital principally from large personal or corporate gifts, and can use their income for special projects or to fill gaps in the flow of current giving. The history of these foundations can be traced back to 1913, but again take-off has been principally from the late 1970s. One factor in this was a new enterpreneurial approach: not 'creeping ahead', as an American informant put it, by trying the accumulate capital out of current revenue, but setting out instead to secure enough capital up front to carry a foundation through to the point where it is established and able to attract new finance in a regular stream.

Company involvement in joint efforts to generate enterprise and regenerate communities has a long history in America, though a spasmodic one: sometimes, as in the recovery of the South from the devastation of the Civil War, it was the community which created the companies rather than the other way round. Here again a new surge of involvement began from the 1960s when, as one report puts it, business was ill-regarded, race riots underlined the problems of urban decay, and 'Chief Executive Officers looked out of their windows and said "If we don't do something this city will cease to be a place where we can do business"'. Business-backed initiatives in Pittsburgh, Minneapolis, Lowell, Baltimore are only some of the best-known examples.

Another significant recent American development has been cooperation between business, local government, and the voluntary sector to create community leadership programmes: joint training programmes, usually lasting a year, to bring together present and up and coming leaders from all sectors in a community, break barriers of ignorance and misunderstanding, and build over time a cadre of local leaders who are aware of each other's and the community's problems and of how they might be tackled. Philadelphia's community leadership programme began in 1959, but real takeoff started in Atlanta in 1969, following a plane crash in which many of the community's younger leaders were killed. By 1979 there were 40 programmes, and by 1988 between 450 and 500.

The Conference Board's report on *The Contributions Function*, while emphasising the variety of ways in which companies manage their contributions function, also notes the link over time between the growth of companies' programmes for community investment and the tendency to rethink their management: starting from 'very small budgets, reflecting the community interests of the chief executive officers, and administered by them as an after-hours activity', and moving on towards more formal structures with specifically assigned personnel, contributions committees or company foundations, and formal plans, budgets, policy statements, and assignment of approval limits. There has been a progressive shift, as one American informant said, from 'an emotive response to charity' to 'systematic philanthropy' and a search for 'efficient' giving.

So, again, the general point is clear. The culture of giving in American corporations has not always been as it is now. It has grown over several decades, with pauses and accelerations, sometimes moving faster on one front than another, as when United Ways continued to spread while the overall level of giving by corporations was on a plateau. It has been a long haul: but also with the encouraging finding that development can be sharply speeded up when the conditions are right.

What, in that case, does American experience show to be the right conditions for progress? The story here has a double point, about the significance of national influences, but the primary importance of personal initiatives and contacts and of more or less formal networks.

National influences matter
National influences and the national climate have certainly mattered. There are some intriguing sidelines. Though, for example, America does not have royalty, the official history of the United Way is careful to print the photograph of every President since Calvin Coolidge handing over his personal cheque. But the main national influences have been of three kinds.

The climate of government and enterprise
In the first place, the plateau of corporate giving in the decades after the Second World War, and the surge in the 1980s, have an obvious explanation in the shift in national policies and the national climate first towards 'big government' and then away from it, as awareness of the limits of government action and of the case for encouraging initiatives by the private and voluntary sector grew.

'Big government', as it developed in America as well as Britain in the decades after the Second World War, did not necessarily prevent business initiatives in the community, but neither did it particularly encourage them. It is easy to think of British examples. The local enterprise agencies which shot up and flourished in the 1930s disappeared from view when the government took over location of industry policy after 1950. Paper II quotes the view of managers in the major shareholding institutions in 1985 that in our 'highly taxed welfare state' company giving is marginalised and per cent giving would never take off: an outdated view by that time, but a fair summary of experience in earlier years. On the American side, it is not surprising that the level of corporate giving stagnated from the 1950s to the 1970s, and took off again only when the deficiencies of 'big government' became apparent and, as in Britain, the political climate correspondingly changed. The record of several of the recent American initiatives listed above shows that they sprang from growing awareness among business people, as among others, of unsolved problems in local communities, and of the difficulty of getting the necessary action through government alone or by leaving government (local or national) and other agencies to operate in separate compartments. The Conference Board underlines the importance for company involvement of the Reagan administration's 'New Federalism' and its expression in the report of the President's task force on private sector initiatives.

Profitability had an influence on companies' readiness to respond to the new trend, though with a delayed reaction, and in the end with a tendency to put on the brakes. Real profits were high in 1977-80, and a rise in the percentage of pre-tax profits donated followed in the early and middle 1980s. After 1981 real profits fell, but again companies' reaction was delayed: a modest fall in the percentage donated became apparent only after 1985, in what the Conference Board report for 1987 called 'this era of cost-cutting and re-structuring'.

It is important, however, to be clear what the response of business to the new climate of the early 1980s did not imply. It was not a case of business setting out to replace government in what were still seen as government's main roles. Business could not have done so, for corporate contributions were still only a minimal fraction of government expenditure: about 5 per cent, for one comparison, of expenditure on non-defence goods and services by the federal government alone. But neither had businesses any intention of doing so. The community investment programmes of individual companies remained, as has been shown, individual, and when they are averaged it is clear that the priorities of American businesses remained those of business, and different from those which might be expected of government. The great bulk of educational donations, for example, continued to go to higher education, and not least to the prestige colleges. Less than one tenth as much went, at least directly, to pre-college education, in spite of the very real problems being experienced by many American high schools. Housing is a major problem in many American cities, but the Conference Board's respondents in 1987 contributed just $6.5 million towards it, 0.4 per cent of their total donations. When businesses increased their contributions in the 1980s it was, to borrow a phrase from our Hillingdon case study, to add more icing to the cake, not to replace the government cake itself.

The law and taxation
A much longer-running national influence has been the contribution of the government and the courts to smoothing the way for American companies' giving through the law and taxation.

The law on charitable giving by corporations was clarified in the 1930s and 1950s. Great donors in the nineteenth century like Carnegie and Rockefeller gave away their own money, but by the 1920s it was accepted that corporations as such could properly make charitable donations out of their shareholders' funds if the donations were of direct benefit to the company or its employees. In 1935 Congress removed the direct benefit condition and made charitable donations tax-deductible up to 5 per cent of pre-tax profits: this was raised to 10 per cent in 1981. Some doubts about *ultra vires* remained after 1935, but in 1953 these were removed in a landmark decision of the Supreme Court of New Jersey, arising out of objection by a shareholder to a grant to a university, not for specific benefit to the company or its employees, but for the university's general purposes. The court concluded that under modern conditions corporations have the power to make reasonable charitable contributions even without specific authorisation by statute or the company's certificate of incorporation. Companies, in effect, could be deemed to have a general purposes clause such as has been proposed in Britain by George Goyder, 'to act towards the community of which it is a member in as responsible a manner as would be expected from a responsible citizen in the like circumstances'.

Tax incentives for corporate giving have also played a part. British and American tax incentives are not now very different, but one major type of incentive, tax-deductibility for one-off (non-covenanted) gifts, was introduced in America much earlier. For companies it was introduced in Britain (Paper II) only in 1986 – for close companies only in 1990 – and for individuals only in 1987 for GAYE and in 1990 for other giving: and still provided that the 'other' gift is at least £600, whereas in America there is no minimum. In America as in Britain, tax incentives have had a mixed press. Harry Kidd, in field visits for the Charities Aid Foundation in 1985,[4] found a contrast between what the literature said and what American corporation officers told him. In one study, 47 per cent of companies questioned had said that the importance of tax incentives was substantial: but 'company officers in oral discussion tell me otherwise', and in any case, Kidd pointed out, 47 per cent is less than half. He concluded nevertheless that tax-deductibility at least removed a hindrance to giving and was an indicator of public support for it: if nothing else, it raised a flag.

The ideology of corporate responsibility: the stakeholder concept
A third important national influence in America has been the relatively early acceptance into management ideology, in its literature as well as its practice, of the concept of the corporation as responsible to various 'stakeholders', one of which is the community. The 1953 New Jersey decision clarifying companies' right to contribute to the community was influenced among other things by strong testimony by business leaders to the effect that companies and the communities where they operate are interdependent, and that it is good practice for individual businesses, and in the general interest of private enterprise, to acknowlege this interdependence and avoid disappointing the reasonable expectations which follow from it. Statements of this kind run through the history of corporate giving in America. They are not actually very different from those made by leading British companies, and fit easily enough into what a previous PSI report[5] identified as the 'new management culture' which has been developing in Britain in recent years. But, as with tax incentives, America was ahead: the

4   H. Kidd, *Companies, Charity, and Tax: USA and UK*, Charities Aid Foundation, 1985.

5   M.P. Fogarty and D. Brooks, *Trade Unions and British Industrial Development*, PSI 1986: 2nd extended edition 1989.

stakeholder concept entered into American management ideology earlier and more widely than in Britain.

But personal and local initiative has mattered most

It would be quite wrong, however, to think of the rise of the culture of giving among American corporations primarily in terms of national influences. It is impossible to follow the history of corporate giving in the United States without realising that the chief way in which it has grown and spread has been through personal and local initiative, influenced by example, consolidated through associations and systematic promotion, but always coming back to person to person contacts and networking, particularly but not only at top management level: between companies, within companies, and between companies and other public or voluntary agencies.

The case histories on the rise of community leadership programmes presented in *A Colorful Quilt* are as good an example as any. In Birmingham, Alabama, the president and vice-president of the Chamber of Commerce 'decided it was time to address the problem of Birmingham's leadership', commissioned a review of leadership programmes elsewhere, and assembled a steering committee headed by the chairman of an insurance company. In Philadephia the idea of community leadership seminars 'was conceived in 1957 primarily by three men': a lawyer with previous experience in local government and as a director of a local development agency, a bank president, and the director of an institute of government studies at the University of Pennsylvania. In Rhode Island a staff member in the Greater Providence Chamber of Commerce alerted its president to the possibilities of leadership programmes, and the president then brought in among others a banker as chairman of a steering committee and the head of the state AFL/CIO as a member. In San Diego, California, the story is that three of the city's most active and visible business leaders ran across each other for the third time in a week at a community affairs meeting, began to wonder 'Aren't there more community leaders out there?', and took the initiative accordingly through the board of the local United Way.

Local and informal networks lead on into others which are wider and more formal, but it is still the local networks which count most. The community leadership movement was consolidated in 1979 through the formation of a National Association of Community Leadership Organisations, but the drive still came from the bottom. United Way, similarly, had a period of major consolidation, including incidentally the adoption of a common name, at the end of the 1960s and the start of the 1970s, but after as before the force of the movement lay in the 2,200 local

United Ways and their network of voluntary officers, company secondees, and volunteers.

At the end of the day the overwhelming impression from American experience is that the culture of giving spreads primarily because people go out and talk to other people, get them together round issues immediately visible and interesting to them, and get something going, after which osmosis operates, the patch of oil spreads, and eventually consolidation into formal associations, systematic promotion, and a national trend follow. National influences have been important, but the process of developing the culture of giving in America has been first and foremost polycentric and bottom-up, through initiatives by people in business, local authorities, voluntary agencies, colleges and universities: and always, so far as companies are concerned, starting from where a company actually is and allowing for the diversity of companies' circumstances and interests.

The implications of relying so much on detailed person to person contacts and local initiatives, however, should not be misunderstood. This is not a formula for petty steps. Even on a local scale, another message from American case histories is: think big, plan properly, build back-up behind local initiatives, manage professionally (even if part-time), and go to the top for leadership and resources, through people who have access to executive suites. The Americans have not been timid in promoting the culture of giving. As the American informant quoted above said from his own experience in developing community foundations: be entrepreneurial: think in terms of several million dollars up front – $5 million was his suggestion for Britain – if a foundation is to reach autonomous take-off after five to seven years. Or, to take even a relatively small scale activity: the typical budget for a community leadership progamme in one small city might be £25-35,000 a year, and in a larger one like Philadelphia £150-200,000.

Conclusion

The lessons of American experience for Britain can be put in terms of particular examples of company community involvement which we might wish to follow, as is in fact happening: in urban regeneration and enterprise development, targeted hiring, federated giving, volunteering from the workplace, community leadership programmes, community trusts and foundations, or styles of managing the 'contributions function'. But this chapter has focussed on the process by which the culture of giving among American corporations has developed, and on this there are four main findings.

- *Companies' individual situations and interests must be respected.* Averages make readable history, but companies' market and community circumstances, interests, and potential for community investment are individual. There can be conventions about good practice, as in the Per Cent Clubs, but there is no standard pattern which fits all companies: the message about community investment has to be tailored to each company's own case. Even 'company' may be too wide a term, for in a multi-unit company circumstances differ from one unit to another.

- *The message about corporate giving passes primarily through personal, one-to-one, contacts and networking*, with the qualification, as has been said, that it is important not to take this as a reason for thinking small. The establishment of national associations and promotional organisations may and does follow, but their role is still to promote and provide back-up for the personal initiatives and formal or informal networks through which development has in the end to proceed.

- *Nation-wide influences are nevertheless important*: whether they take the form of creating a climate in which the need for and potential of business investment in the community is recognised and business leaders are motivated to respond, of removing legal and fiscal obstacles to company giving, or of shaping and diffusing an ideology of corporate responsibility in the community, as part of a wider 'stakeholder' concept of the company. Always, however, with the reservation, related to the finding about respect for companies' individual circumstances, that the priorities of business are priorities as perceived by business, and not necessarily the same as those of public authorities: still less a bid to take over public authorities' responsibilities.

- *The long haul can be accelerated.* Diffusing and maintaining a culture of giving in a large and changing population of companies, each with its individual circumstances and potential, through the very personal and decentralised processes which carry the message best, is in American experience a long haul: in the crisp comment of one of our British informants, 'bloody hard work'. But the pace of development in America has not been uniform. American experience shows how it can be accelerated. In the right national climate the processes of personal contact and networking can be galvanised, as happened from the mid-1970s onwards, into a flow of new initiatives and a new level of overall performance: which is precisely the problem to which this report is addressed in the case of Britain.

Note: The United Way[6]
Purpose

'A local United Way is a non-profit, non-governmental, private voluntary organisation. It raises local donations for member health and human welfare charities'. 'It is a most efficient system of fund raising...so the recipient charities can focus their trained efforts on providing service'. 10 per cent of receipts, typically, go towards overheads, the other 90 per cent being distributed directly to the recipient charities.

'Corporate giving, year-round payroll giving, special events, and other special fund-raising activities should be major goals for United Ways', and 'maximising resources, efficient use of volunteer hours, and low fund-raising costs are major United Way benefits'.

Organisations seeking United Way support should be incorporated as charities, with a volunteer board, provide a needed service in the community, and have both a balanced budget and audited accounts. A United Way should publish the standards on which it admits new organisations and programmes to support, give each organisation requesting funds 'a specific opportunity to present its case', and set the goal of each campaign according to 'the need for services, past performance of givers, and the current climate for fund raising'.

Many United Ways also provide information and referral services. 'A computerised data base is maintained on health and human welfare services in the community', and can be referred to by anyone.

United Ways are expected:

> To work with other sectors (for example government, other non-profit organisations, and local business and labour leadership) to ensure that the population's human needs are being addressed. It is the responsibility of the planning segment of United Way organisations to identify needs in the community and, if necessary, bring to the attention of the Board services that are not available.

United Ways should also work with other institutions, programmes, and organisations to eliminate unnecessary overlap and duplication of services.

Constitution

A United Way should be incorporated as a private non-profit voluntary organisation. The 'membership body' should be clearly identified in the

---

6   From *Suggested Standards for United Way Organizations*, United Way International, 1989, and correspondence with United Way International.

constitution. It should have 'representation from diverse elements of the population and various constituencies, including givers and possibly some service agency representatives', with no discrimination on grounds of race or national origin, sex, or politics. The 'membership body' elects the Board, which in turn elects the officers and may elect other committees, such as an Executive or Allocations Committee. There should be a nominating committee to propose a slate of candidates for the Board: candidates 'should have demonstrated leadership in the community and be able to assure financial and programme success of the United Way'. They should also represent 'all walks of life (business, clergy, civic, etc.)'. Board members should rotate, perhaps on the basis of one third retiring each year, and should not normally hold office for more than two three year terms. Officers should not normally hold a given office for more than two years. Board members are unpaid, and professional staff should not be members of the Board.

Administration

'Every United Way organisation needs a clear statement of mission, including goals and objectives against which its progress can be measured by the community'. Budgets must be balanced, and professionally audited accounts published. Larger United Ways have paid staff, but smaller ones may have only volunteers. In any case there should be a chief professional officer appointed by the Board, and held accountable for hiring and staff performance.

Publicity

'Most people are motivated to give because of their concern for others. Therefore, United Ways must convey to contributors their concern for helping people and their ability to help solve human problems'. The media and community should be kept informed 'on a year-round basis'. United Ways should also make clear their identification with United Way International and use its logo.

Relation of local to national/international United Ways

'The role of the national organisation... should be to assist local United Ways in improving their own capacity': but local United Ways in turn are expected to live up to the movement's centrally agreed *Suggested Standards*. United Way International 'by incorporating these standards in its licensing agreements authorising the use of the name and logo, reserves the right to revoke same in the event these standards are not met'.

Appendix

Details of postal survey

- 300 questionnaires were sent; 120 valid replies were received, giving a 40 per cent response rate.
- The sample was chosen randomly from the EXTEL database of firms making donations to charities; firms were chosen which came within the size range 500-2999 employees. A few respondents fell outside this range due to the age of some of the entries on the EXTEL database; they have not been excluded from the analysis.
- Unbracketed numbers below show total responses; numbers in brackets give percentage of respondent sample.

Sample profile:

- Industry sector:

Manufacturing/extraction	-	63	(52.5)
Services/construction	-	55	(45.8)
Not answered	-	1	(1.7)
Size range in UK:			
1-499	-	11	(9.2)
500-999	-	32	(26.7)
1000-1999	-	45	(37.5)
2000-2999	-	24	(20.0)
3000 +	-	8	(6.6)

- Ownership

Independent UK	-	68	(56.7)
UK group	-	14	(11.7)
US group	-	22	(18.3)
other overseas	-	12	(10.0)
public sector	-	4	(3.3)

- Turnover in UK (£ million)

under 0.5	-	2	(1.7)
0.5 - 0.99	-	0	(0.0)
1 - 9.9	-	3	(2.5)
10 - 49.9	-	21	(17.5)
50 - 100	-	36	(30.0)
over 100	-	57	(47.5)
not answered	-	1	(0.8)